Pieces of my Mind

Brendan Hoban

BANLEY
HOUSE

Published by Banley House,
40 Ormond Road, Rathmines, Dublin 6.
© 2007

ISBN 978-0-9540337-1-2

For

Áine, Bethan, Caoimhe, Cian

Pieces of my Mind

Brendan Hoban

CONTENTS

Other books by Brendan Hoban

Personally Speaking
(1995)

The Lisnagoola Chronicles
(1995))

Sermons for Special Occasions
(1997)

A Touch of the Heart
(2002)

Change or Decay
(2004)

A private, individual spirituality that depends on an individual's resources and the limited narrative of their own experience hasn't the language or the scaffolding needed to stand its ground or survive in the real world. And what happens is that it either degenerates into some form of self-indulgent ego-tripping or it loses itself in tree-hugging or some such specious nonsense.

Making your own soup

Fr Peter Connolly, Professor of English in Maynooth many years ago, once confided to a friend that, at some point in the future, the practice of the Catholic religion in Ireland could collapse suddenly. What was remarkable about this statement was that it was made in the 1960s, a time when the Catholic Church in Ireland was at the peak of its power and influence: over 90% attended church; seminaries were full; the credibility of bishops and clergy couldn't be higher; and so on.

When asked why he had arrived at what now seems an extraordinarily prescient and prophetic conclusion, Connolly replied that the Irish are not a sentimental people, 'once they find something is not useful, they abandon it.'

One of the more obvious things about religious practice in the Irish Catholic Church is that while there has been significant leakage in every age group, young adults are conspicuous by their absence from church now. And if you ask them, why they don't go to Mass, almost invariably the answer is around their conviction that 'it doesn't do anything for me'. It is, to them, not *useful*.

It's not that they are, generally speaking, anti-church. In the main, they retain a respect for the religious enterprise and those involved with it; they understand how precious to their parents and to some of their own generation is their religious heritage; and they can see how, as a social imperative, religion helps to sustain important social values. But, it doesn't do anything for them at a personal level, so they look away.

This decline, if that's the word for it, follows an almost identical pattern throughout the developed world. It's happening in Britain, the continent of Europe, Australia and the United States. Bring a group of young adults together in any of these societies, even from family backgrounds where religious practice was a core value, and you find the same thing, a disconnection with the religion of their parents.

And side by side with that, you find an interest in and sympathy with the importance of spirituality. As interest in 'religion' diminishes, correspondingly interest in 'spirituality' seems to grow. And ask them what they mean by 'spirituality' and they will begin by defining it as having nothing to do with 'religion' which more and more they seem to define as mere church-going. Spirituality, as they see it, is a sense of connection with God that is different from and separate from what they see happening in church on a Sunday morning: it's personal, private, free from structures, connecting with 'where we're at'.

Some people, parents usually, are relieved and a bit consoled by their adult children's interest in spirituality, often on the basis that at least the baby hasn't been thrown out with the bathwater. Parents tend to say that their adult children are 'good people', have strong values (especially in the area of justice) and have their own belief in God. And all of that is true.

But my difficulty is that a private, individual spirituality that depends on an individual's resources and the limited narrative of their own experience hasn't the language or the scaffolding needed to stand its ground or survive in the real world. And what happens is that it either degenerates into some form of self-indulgent ego-tripping or it loses itself in tree-hugging or some such specious nonsense.

I have a number of difficulties with some of the newer versions of personal spirituality. One is that while it can be talked about at great length, sometimes it doesn't happen at all. It never actually gets done. Another is that it's a half-way house to disbelief, in two forms: one is that it suits people who don't want to name their disinterest and eventually disbelief in God; and, two, it bounces the following generation into disbelief because there's nothing to hold on to, no language of worship, no sense of ritual, no scaffolding of religion - even to react against. If everyone ends up making their own soup, inevitably the gruel becomes thinner and thinner.

The other great difficulty I have with people doing their own thing in religion - in the sense of the human encounter with the divine - is that the personal becomes isolated from the communal. Faith is a personal journey but religion is, of its essence, about relating to what is outside ourselves - God, other people, the world.

The problem we have now is that the public expression of our religion - worship in church as a community (or Mass on the weekend) - no longer feeds the spirit of a generation operating more and more out of a faithless culture. And we're left with the young making up their own spirituality on the run.

Which is where Peter Connolly came in. Because the narrative of the past and the scaffolding that sustained it are so out of sync with the needs of a new generation, they are being discarded because they are experienced as of no *use*. We are failing to open up new avenues into the great Catholic heritage and history will not be kind to us for that omission.

We need to listen to what the young are saying to us through their non-participation. Otherwise they may well be the last generation to have 'the faith'.

There's a sadness in the thirtysomethings that despite their education, money, lifestyle and resources they sense the need for a spirituality that would put some shape on the lives they lead. They are searching for, indeed hungry for, a meaning that would, as one of them put it, help them to find 'a place to go to when I realise there aren't people who can fix things.' A place where the questions at the heart of life might be reflectively considered.

Thirty somethings

SOME time ago, in *The Irish Times*, there was a poem by Gerard Hanberry called *Bravado*. The poem is a reaction to a conversation with a friend about life, death, the hereafter. Hanberry dismisses his friend's nonchalance in the face of distant death. When the time comes, his friend suggests, he will 'invite the good Padre with his mumbo-jumbo to be off with himself'.

Hanberry doesn't accept this. He tells his friend that 'they got to you young' and that as a result he has been humping a 'rucksack of guilt' since childhood. When the time comes and his friend is facing the darkness, Hanberry believes, he will be 'trying to work out some policy for the hereafter'.

You could imagine Gerard Hanberry and his friend having a drink in a pub and the conversation drifting towards the big questions and eventually they find themselves mulling over death.

I don't know what age they are but I'd bet that they're in the thirty-something category. They've gone to college, married, changed a few cars, did the prescribed gig to Australia (complete with rucksack), came home, got married, bought a house, had a few kids and now find themselves trying to work out what it's all about. Hanberry's generation, find themselves, in Hanberry's phrase to his friend, 'scanning the ultrasound printout of your own mortality'.

The thirtysomethings are searching for something. They don't know what it is but they sense that it isn't what their mothers are telling them they need: believe in God, go to Mass, teach your children to pray, live with the mystery. They are being offered a religion but what they suspect they need is a spirituality.

They find that they are uncomfortable with their parents' attitudes and values. They react against the accepting, almost credulous approach of their parents – the priest said it so it must be right – as their gut-reaction is to question. They simply don't believe truths that their parents just accept without reflection.

When they go to Mass they find the ritual formal and unsatisfying. It doesn't engage them. It is as if it speaks a language they no longer understand. They find too that priests lack the reflective capacity 'to say something', to connect with where they are. For a while they persevere out of loyalty to the food of their youth or the promptings of a parent or unease that they may be letting down their children.

But gradually they leave the Church behind, airbrushing it out of their lives, apart from the inconvenience and awkwardness of First Communions or Confirmations. The Church is for them now – in a world where so much seems so relative – still too sharp, too arrogant, too sure of itself. Everything is too neatly packaged and some of it makes no sense. And, with the scandals of clerical child sexual abuse, they have lost faith in the Church's capacity to reform itself, to learn a different language. So they give themselves permission to defect from its concerns.

Yet, in the small hours, they wonder about life and death and whether they should be giving their children something more substantial than karate or ballet lessons?

There's a sadness in the thirtysomethings that despite their education, money, lifestyle and resources they sense the need for a spirituality that would put some shape on the lives they lead. They are searching for, indeed hungry for, a meaning that would, as one of them put it, help them to find 'a place to go to when I realise there aren't people who can fix things.' A place where the questions at the heart of life might be reflectively considered.

What they seek is a scaffolding to hold a meaning that they sense is at the heart of life. They have felt the weight and texture of life. They have a keen sense of what it is to be authentic. They know what they are looking for but no one seems to be able to provide it.

On the few occasions they find themselves at Mass they hear poor sermons set in a disorganised liturgy and all it does is convince them that the Church is not the place where they will find what they are looking for. They want a liturgy that speaks to them about the concerns of their lives – and if they could get what they're looking for they would drive a hundred miles every weekend to savour it.

When, like Gerard Hanberry's friend, they have a few drinks on them, the thirtysomethings can find themselves dismissing religion and Church as, in Hanberry's phrase, 'all that medieval twaddle.' But in their more reflective moments they realise that you can't just glibly dismiss centuries of ritual and tradition – anymore than you can justify going off meat for life because the local butcher hasn't got his act together. Especially when, as the years roll by, they begin to experience the gap the loss of a spirituality opens up in their lives and they begin to suspect that they're mutating into younger versions of their fathers and mothers.

The thirtysomethings are a lost generation, suspended in an in-between world, happy enough to shed their religious affiliation but perplexed by their ongoing hunger for meaning and a spirituality at the heart of life. And sometimes too, wondering what the loss will mean for them and for their children.

Many Catholics today find themselves living their lives at a distance from the Church. And then when they present themselves to a priest to organise a wedding or to baptise a baby, they can feel vulnerable and uneasy. They know and the priest knows that they don't 'practice' and their antennae are sensitively tuned into any signal that might be interpreted as unacceptance or even rejection on the part of the priest.

The less rules the better

In *The Tablet*, Daniel O'Leary, a priest in Yorkshire, England, described an encounter he had with a young Catholic couple from 'a good Catholic family' who asked to be married in his church. He had never seen them at Mass so he suggested that maybe he should meet them again to chat about it. He never saw them again and word drifted back to him about the perception in the parish that he was 'a hard man'. 'I now know, in my heart' he writes 'that I was wrong'.

I think many priests have instances like that which, in retrospect and in pain, they regret. It could be the tone of voice or a bad day or a casual insensitivity but afterwards you know that you got it wrong and the regret seeps in at the edges.

In recent years, pastoral situations have become more complicated and more problematic for the priest. And priests have to manage them with as much sensitivity and tact as possible: irregular marriage situations, the baptism of children whose parents no longer believe; the reception of Communion in theologically awkward situations; and so on.

Like the politician who once said that in an ideal world the best run hospitals would be ones without any patients, in parish life everything can seem utterly clear in a theoretical sense, but once you begin to apply a rule to real life complexity and confusion can abound.

Parish life comes out of a tradition where rules were everything. Now often we don't know what to do when the rules don't seem to make much sense anymore. An understandable knee-jerk reaction is to issue a series of diocesan regulations that govern problematic areas: music at weddings; who can be a sponsor at baptism; panegyrics at funeral Masses; and so.

I'm not too sure that devising a whole shaft of new rules to cover every possible situation is all that helpful at all, apart maybe from allowing the individual priest to blame the bishop.

Rules or more rules or no rules don't absolve the priest at local level from the difficulty of 'managing' each situation as it presents itself. The truth is, that every situation is different and needs to be assessed in conjunction with those involved in a non-contentious and collaborative way. And quoting a rule to defend a position often causes more bother than its worth.

Many Catholics today find themselves living their lives at a distance from the Church. And then when they present themselves to a priest to organise a wedding or to baptise a baby, they can feel vulnerable and uneasy. They know and the priest knows that they don't 'practice' - in the sense of weekly worship - and their antennae are sensitively tuned into any signal that might be interpreted as unacceptance or even rejection on the part of the priest.

What they need is someone who will respond to them in a quiet, accepting mode. What they don't want is someone quoting the latest regulations at them, which they perceive as yet another obstacle Mother Church has placed in their way. And the result is that, like the couple in Daniel O'Leary's example mentioned above, they just walk away, with everyone losing out, the couple, their children and the Church, to which in some way they want to continue to belong but are now even more alienated than they were.

The truth of the present pastoral scene is that many who continue to regard themselves as Catholics, who still feel they want to belong to the Catholic family, often have little or no contact with the Church apart from baptisms, weddings and funerals. The result is that these occasions have become central in the life of parishes because how the Church, in the person of the priest, manages such occasions, carries a huge weight.

My own view is that the more we multiply rules and regulations - and I'm not saying that we should have no rules, because we have to have rules - the more unbending we may become. And the more unbending we are *perceived* to become. Most problems and difficulties can be sorted out if a priest and his parishioners sit down in an accepting, non-judgmental and non-combative context and see what, with a bit of give and take, can be worked out. Rules and regulations never cover every possible eventuality. And, sometimes, the one obstruction to an amenable compromise is yet another rule-book that someone somewhere imagined would be helpful.

Priests are often the first point of contact people have with the Church. And we often get it wrong. Getting it right isn't about handing us another sheaf of rules but helping us to meet the alienated and disaffected (and not just them) with something of the acceptance and compassion of the carpenter of Nazareth.

I've never met a priest yet who regretted that he was too compassionate with his people. I've met a lot of priests who regret that they were too strict. And when you talk to them, they (and the rest of us) can relate specific instances which they particularly regret.

Everything works perfectly in theory. Throw a few human beings into the mix - especially if one of them is brandishing a new set of rules and the others expect to be rejected - and everything becomes unstuck. Sometimes we manage things better without too many rules.

I remember someone saying to me one time that he never really believed in God until his first child, a little girl, was born. It wasn't that he disbelieved in God. It was just that, when he reflected on the experience of the birth of his child, somehow things began to slot into place. He realised too that while we can explain in scientific or other terms the mechanics of reproduction and birth, the gift of life is a miraculous, unquantifiable extra.

Rumours of God

*O*N *Coronation Street,* a character called Norris was sitting at the hospital bedside of his friend Emily, who was unconscious. Norris said that he felt helpless, that there was nothing he could do for Emily. He would, he said, have liked to pray for Emily but that when he tried to pray he often found that he got no response so he gave it up.

I think that's the experience of many. We find prayer difficult because when we pray, when we talk to God, often we don't get any direct or tangible response. There's no echo, no resonance to our words or thoughts. It's as if they just disappear into thin air and we're left sitting there or kneeling there with nothing to show for it.

But even though that experience can be frustrating and difficult and off-putting, it's what we have to expect when we talk to God. We can't link up with God the way we link up with people because there is between the divine and the human an almost unbridgeable gap.

Prayer isn't about trying to get God to take up the phone. It's about putting ourselves into a mood or an atmosphere where we can pick up rumours of God's presence with us. No more than that.

I remember someone saying to me one time that he never really believed in God until his first child, a little girl, was born. It wasn't that he disbelieved in God. It was just that, when he reflected on the experience of the birth of his child, somehow things began to slot into place. He realised, for instance, in a way he never had before, how deeply his own parents loved him. He realised too that while we can explain in scientific or other terms the mechanics of reproduction and birth, the gift of life is a miraculous, unquantifiable extra.

Ultimately I think that the quest for God is about searching for threads of the divine in the tapestry of human experience. There is a deeper truth behind what we actually see or feel or touch. As in the tapestry itself what we see is not what actually holds it together. When we look at a tapestry, we see thousands of horizontal threads making up a great design. But what we can't see are the vertical supports that actually sustain the whole tapestry.

I think life, in a sense, is a bit like a vast tapestry. The design gradually emerges and we need both time and a sense of perspective to take it in. We have to stay with it and we have to stand back from it. And often when we have key experiences in life - falling in love, the death of a spouse, a baby being born or whatever - an important part of the design of life gets filled in and we begin to get glimpses of threads of the divine emerging. We pick up a rumour of God.

Religion ultimately is a search for God. For some there is a happy clarity and a natural resonance that lead them to a green and fertile valley. For others, there are only vague and distant echoes that lead to frustrating and lonely paths into desert places; and the rest of us pilgrim somewhere between those extremes.

And we search in different ways: in the reading of his word in the Scriptures, in the breaking of bread, in the communion we experience in community worship, in the Communion we receive in the Eucharist, in the experience of loving those closest to us in the world and not least in a reflective presence that senses a deeper truth behind the ordinariness of a lived life.

But because the gap is so wide between the human and the divine we find it difficult a lot of the time to uncover the presence of God, to feel, to experience that echo or that resonance with God.

Now if we want to find threads of the divine in the tapestry of our own experience, we have to see prayer not as making a phone-call to God but a way of being receptive to God's presence in our lives. And that needs space and time and, above all, the ability to listen. It's responding to the call of Jesus in the gospel when he says: *Come and see.*

The gift of God is in the call. Not everyone gets that call, not everyone has faith. But the tragedy is that, for so many, the call is there and we don't hear it. It's not that God isn't speaking to us, but that because we've allowed our lives to become so cluttered up with work and recreation and noise and people, we're not able to find the threads of the divine in the tapestry of our own lives.

We can be so busy that we have little time and space and thought for reflecting on our experience, for seeking and searching for a God who continues to knock at the door of our hearts and like Samuel in the Old Testament we can't make out what it means even when we here the rumours.

Ultimately, I think, we eventually learn that all that matters in life is being able to hear the right voices.

Part of our difficulty as a church is that we come out of an old world that we somehow believe we can re-create in another age. We can't. We can no more go back to the way we were than we can put toothpaste back into a tube. And every time a church leader gives the impression of being ill-at-ease in this new world by being narrow or intolerant or authoritarian in his views, he is cutting off another budding shoot of the church of the new millennium that is struggling to flower

Something is dying

IN *The Irish Times*, the poet, Aidan Mathews, wrote 'Something in my tradition is dying and something is being born.' He finds the change in small things: a priest's number in the directory is now listed in the business section; five hundred girls pour out of a playground and not one of them answers to the name Mary; at a crowded Requiem Mass the altar-boy with Down's Syndrome is a sole guide for the cultural Christians on when to stand, when to kneel, what to say; and the thirty-somethings buying their houses look at Sacred Heart pictures and Child of Prague statues 'with all the courtesy and incomprehension they'd direct at Polynesian face-masks in the Chester Beatty Library.'

You can see what he means. The new Ireland was mesmerised a few years ago when An Taoiseach and representatives of the government formally greeted Cardinal Connell on his arrival back from Rome at Dublin Airport. For us oldies, the deference of State to Church was a natural part of the way we were.

The old order is changing, making way for the new. In terms of society, we are at present balanced on a scales. Sometimes we tilt towards the old Ireland based loosely on its Catholic nationalist ethos, where people go to Mass on Sunday, defer to the authority of the church, have traditional moral and political allegiances and feel at home in that narrow world of the past where everything seemed more insular, more settled and more secure. And sometimes we tilt towards a new and different Ireland where religion is a matter of private choice, where personal freedom is paramount, where equality and civility and modernity are key words and where openness, tolerance and acceptance are key themes.

There is a lot in most of us hankering after the past. It is about identity, place, rootedness, familiarity: being at home, feeling the clay under our feet, knowing the words. Corpus Christi processions, Latin Mass, Benediction on a Sunday evening, relics, Confession on a Saturday night, the Sodalities and the Pope coming to Knock - all confirming a view of the world that would last forever.

Now many see the Papal Mass in the Phoenix Park as part of a great funeral liturgy for the dying of an old world. A new threshold has been crossed and a new and different world is born. The present economic boom and the transformation of Irish society that attends it is the creation in the main of a young population, educated, vibrant, creative, open-minded and tolerant. The problem for the Church is that it insists on giving the impression that it is out of tune with that new world: old, narrow, intolerant, authoritarian.

Part of our difficulty as a church is that we come out of an old world that we somehow believe we can re-create in another age. We can't. We can no more go back to the way we were than we can put toothpaste back into a tube. And every time a church leader gives the impression of being ill-at-ease in this new world by criticising a sister church or being narrow or intolerant or authoritarian in his views, he is cutting off another budding shoot of the church of the new millennium that is struggling to flower.

Church leaders can even be given marks (or give themselves marks) for 'strong leadership' and for being faithful to the old when, in effect, what they're doing is making it more difficult for faith in Jesus Christ to find new forms in a new age. The young people know that. Their parents, who hear what their teenagers and adult children are saying, know that. And the dogs in the street are even picking it up.

But our church seems to have a particular difficulty in seeing the largest of large writing on the largest of large walls. And there is a growing body of Catholics in Ireland, lay and clerical, who are frustrated and embarrassed and sometimes humiliated by our church's failure to read the sign of the times.

The past is over. That Church, as we knew it in the past, is dying. The old ways are now ancient history and a new and different church has to be given life and energy in a new and different world. And all the pontificating bishops in the world, all the rabid refugees from the past egging them on, all the running around after relics and miracles and Marian visions, all the narrowness, insularism, triumphalism, and smallness of vision, intellect and heart: all of that is simply helping to convince a new generation - educated, emancipated, tolerant, open and ultimately well-disposed to the authentic and the real - that religion is out of tune with the lives they live.

What an unspeakable tragedy. The great breadth of our Catholic tradition and the life-enhancing and life-enriching spirituality that goes with it is being shuffled to the margins of Irish life because we are caught in the binds of the past. And religion, which society badly needs to help carry morality into a new world, becomes no more than a faded black-and-white photograph from a distant past.

Aidan Mathews is right. Something is dying and something is being born. What is dying is a mind-set that defines 'church' in one set of terms and can see no other. And that ensures that a new generation that refuses to accept that mind-set will simply walk away from it. When will we ever learn?

Isn't it a wonderful time to be a Catholic now, as the future opens up all kinds of possibilities. If you doubt that just look at where we've been. Remember when we were told that it was a mortal sin to eat a rasher on a Friday or to tell a risque joke – grave matter, after all! It was all about rules and regulations, subservience and obedience. Then we were told to grow up. That, in effect, was what the Second Vatican Council meant.

No future in the past

A constant mantra today is that everything is changing and that all we can be sure of is that everything will keep changing. Some people are frightened by this, preferring to put the wagons in a circle and to try to keep change at bay. Trying, Canute-like, to keep the tide out and finding themselves holding grimly to some jagged rock with the seas of change threatening to envelope them. Others embrace change, seeing freedom and possibility and life in the changing patterns of life today.

I'm in the second constituency. I believe that this is a wonderful time to be alive. Developments in technology, the prosperity we now enjoy as a people, ease of travel, opportunities for self-development and self-understanding, the personal choices available to people now, the probability of lasting peace in the North, the growing ethos of accountability and transparency in public life, the wonderful educational system we enjoy – are all fuelling change and being fuelled in turn by change. Who in their right minds, I wonder, would want to live in the dismal 1950s in comparison to the land of freedom and opportunity we now enjoy?

The same is true of the Roman Catholic Church. Isn't it a wonderful time to be a Catholic now, as the future opens up all kinds of possibilities. If you doubt that just look at where we've been. Remember when we were told that it was a mortal sin to eat a rasher on a Friday or to tell a risque joke - grave matter, after all! Or for priests not to read the designated breviary within a specified 24 hours, Greenwich-time notwithstanding. It was all about rules and regulations, subservience and obedience. Then we were told to grow up. That, in effect, was what the Second Vatican Council meant. Inevitably there was confusion and insecurity but there was too a glorious sense of freedom and ease. And the greatest freedom of all was the knowledge that change, in terms of church, is not something to be avoided or defined out of existence but the great constant in any institution that wishes to survive and grow.

That's why the recent decision of the Irish Catholic bishops to introduce the ministry of deacons into Irish church life is to be welcomed. Yes, I know that it's limited to men. And yes, like most of the human race, I can't penetrate the mind-set that would demand a celibate commitment if a single man wishes to be a deacon. And I hear what people are saying about the introduction of women deacons.

It's probably too much to accept that the Catholic Church would embrace change. And who would doubt Eric Ericcson's adage about institutions only changing when they have to change? But surely there is a providential imperative of change at work in the Roman Catholic Church now. How else can we make sense of the steep decline in vocations? How else can we understand the unease with the teaching on birth-control among married Catholics? How can we otherwise explain the growing acceptance among the Catholic faithful for a non-celibate priesthood. Or the burgeoning support for the ordination of women? Such realities are both examples and harbingers of seismic change in the Roman Catholic church.

So the decision to ordain married men as deacons is a significant one. There is a domino effect involved here as part of the dynamic of change. For example, when a significant number of Anglican clergy became Roman Catholic priests and began to work in parishes in England, the official position was that this was a peripheral and extraordinary situation, with little real effect on church life. But as those married priests begin to operate in parishes, the normality of a married clergy will gradually be taken for granted. And a decision to ordain married men to priesthood, which is becoming progressively more likely, won't seem as dramatic as heretofore.

The same will happen with married deacons. If a married deacon can baptise his own child or officiate at his daughter's wedding or his mother-in-law's funeral what's the big deal about a married priest saying Mass? And if there are men deacons, why not women deacons? While the Catholic Church at present won't countenance the ordination of women because of perceived theological difficulties, there are no such problems with the ordination of women deacons. After all, in Romans 16:1 Paul refers to Phoebe as the deaconess of the church at Cenchreae.

There seems little doubt but that there were deaconesses in the early church, a crucial consideration, and, we're told that the matter of women deaconesses is under active consideration in Rome at the moment. So it's probably only a matter of time before it becomes acceptable that a woman deacon will baptise her own child or officiate at her son's wedding or her mother-in-law's funeral. And when that happens the ordination of women to the priesthood will seem a logical and natural step.

All part of the great sea-change happening around us. What a wonderful time to be alive. What a wonderful time to be a Roman Catholic. God insists on writing his own script. It's taking us a while to realise that there's no future in the past. But we've getting there - despite ourselves.

*The trick is to acknowledge the reality of change, to plan for change
and to learn to adapt to change. Pulling the wagons in a circle,
blocking out the world we live in is no more than a recipe for
disaster. That much is clear now. Institutions and individuals who
imagine that life can go on as before or that somehow things are
going to settle down soon are living in a make-believe world.*

Clinging to the wreckage

FOR those of us who are the wrong side of fifty, the most
remarkable thing about the lives we've lived is the extraordinary
change we have witnessed in our time. And if anything, the pace of
change is going to increase. Can anyone possibly imagine what life will
be like in fifty, twenty or even ten years time? Everything will be
changed, changed utterly and only God knows what kind of lives we'll
be living.

The trick, we're told, is to acknowledge the reality of change, to
plan for change (if that's now even possible) and to learn to adapt to
change. Pulling the wagons in a circle, blocking out the world we live
in is no more than a recipe for disaster. That much is clear now.
Institutions and individuals who imagine that life can go on as before
or that somehow things are going to settle down soon are living in a
make believe world.

That's particularly true of great institutions struggling to come to
terms with a changing culture. Like the Catholic Church. Forty years
ago, the Church was booming and blooming. It dominated Irish life.
It's influence in Irish society was, in the main, unchallenged. Health
and education and, to a large degree, social affairs were mere
extensions of its spiritual empire. Vocations were teeming and religious

orders were building larger seminaries to cope with them. We had the wind on our backs and we had built up an unassailable lead. Now we're a few goals down, it's the second half and we're playing into the teeth of a bitter gale-force wind. And because we thought nothing would change, we're left floundering with no one, not least our leaders, knowing what to do.

One temptation is to put up the shutters and hope that the storm of change will pass. It won't. There's as much chance of that as there is of the tide not coming in so we have to learn how to swim rather than try to keep the tide at bay. Another temptation is to imagine that we can maintain an oasis of non-change in a maelstrom of change. We can't. We are where we are as a church not just because of Brendan Smyth or Eamon Casey or *States of Fear* or *The Ferns Report* but because of the development of technology, the influence of global media and the information revolution that have fuelled the pace of change. Questions have replaced answers. *Why not?* has replaced *Why?* Possibilities have subsumed limitations. Change is everywhere.

So what can we do? First, I think, we have to accept the reality of what's happening around us. Religion is now peripheral in Irish society because it is now peripheral in most people's lives. We may not like to admit that sad truth but there it is. The fact is that many people have already walked away from the Church and its influence. More are still there in body but their minds are somewhere else and soon they'll be gone too. And many of those who are left behind spend their time giving out about the way we are, obsessively complaining about those in irregular marriage situations, the cost of living and family values and wondering why their self-contained and cosy little world - where everyone knew what a sin was - has imploded.

For this awkward remnant, the anti-dote to the revolution swirling around them is for the clergy to preach the Ten Commandments and for the bishops to reintroduce the old catechism. But the mythical golden age to which they continually refer - if indeed it ever existed - cannot be replicated in a different culture. You can't put the toothpaste back in the tube.

So we have to acknowledge some difficult truths: attendance at weekend Masses will continue to decrease; confession has effectively disappeared; the vast majority of Catholics are uninfluenced by the statements of priest, bishop or Pope; vocations have virtually dried up; and, in the future, the Catholic Church in Irish society will be less significant, less influential, less controlling and hopefully a great deal humbler than it was in the past.

But whatever our history and whatever the circumstances, the work of the church goes on. The good news is that God loves us beyond all our imagining and that experiencing that gives a richness and a texture to our lives that all the money or influence in the world can't provide. It's also about recognising that living life without accepting the spiritual dimension at the heart of all existence is really only partly living. The work of the Church is to mediate these truths in an ever-changing world. That's difficult enough to do without people pretending that nothing has really changed when we're really just clinging to the wreckage of a forgotten past.

The old world is dead and gone. Let's see whether we can be part of the new world.

Whatever we may say about devotions in the past, people knew how to pray. There was a warmth, comfort and directness in our praying that seem to be missing today. While we were occasionally off beam in the past at least our hearts were in the right place. And that's probably at the core of it. Heart, not just head. Poetry, not just prose. Devotions, not just spirituality.

Losing the colour

I don't know if you're old enough to remember a prayer book called *Treasury of the Sacred Heart*. It was very popular in the early part of the last century and was still doing the rounds into the 1960s. It was widely used at Mass and had the Latin text on one side of the page and the English translation on the other, with epistles and gospel readings also in English.

As well as that it had prayers for almost everything under the sun, a host of devotions to a plethora of saints: Novenas, Stations of the Cross, Litanies, the *En Ego*, the *Memorare*, prayers for Benediction, prayers before and after Communion and Confession, prayers for a happy death and so on. Attached to some of these prayers and devotions were a series of indulgences: three-hundred days remission in purgatory for one prayer, four-hundred for another, and the full plenary works for the *En Ego* if you went to Confession and attended Mass, if I remember rightly. If you did the Nine Fridays three times you were half way in the gate of heaven already; if you said *The Thirty Days Prayer* every day for, yes, thirty days you were granted a special favour; and if you had a picture of the Sacred Heart in your house with a red light in front of it your house and family received a special blessing.

At that time our homes were full of holy pictures and statues – Our Lady of Perpetual Succour, The Sacred Heart of Jesus, The Immaculate Heart of Mary, The Child of Prague – all part of the rich and powerful texture of a popular, devotional Catholicism. There was a culture and a vocabulary underpinning a vast range of pious devotions that included the Rosary, sodalities, confraternities, special novenas (like to St Gerard Majella for expectant mothers), brown and white scapulars, the litany of Loretto, prayer to a Guardian Angel and so on.

That kind of folk religion and the devotions that underpinned it have virtually disappeared today. And while we may regret the loss of the warmth and comfort it brought to people, on reflection there was a certain inevitability about its decline: its connection to Scripture was often tenuous; the promises associated with particular devotions often led to a magical approach to prayer; some devotions presented as sentimental and pious in a world becoming increasingly rationalistic; and their private focus ran the risk of disconnection from the centrality of public, community worship.

A case can be made for wondering whether the pendulum has swung too far in the other direction. While the religious devotionalism of the past was often overdone and was open to excess, it gave people a range of prayer-forms to choose from and an ownership over a life of personal prayer. Was it wise, in the aftermath of the Second Vatican Council, to have jettisoned that confident folk tradition that was so much part of the narrative of Catholicism? Would it have been more appropriate to reform its excesses and to situate it more in the context of Scripture and community worship?

The point was made, at the time of the Council, that the devotionalism outlined above developed as a reaction to the exclusion of people from their central role in the Mass. Through the centuries the Mass had been taken over more and more by the priest and the role of the people was to attend rather than participate. It is a measure of people's exclusion from participation in the Mass that priests actually encouraged people to say the Rosary during the Mass or to pray their own private devotions.

While that imbalance had to be set right and while the Mass had to be brought back to the centre of the Christian life for Catholics, maybe now we're in a better position to rediscover forms of individual devotion that can enrich the faith life of individual Catholics. And while many overly-sentimental, cloying and theologically embarrassing devotions had to be set aside, do we now need to discover opportunities for individual and personal devotions that sit more snugly within a broader and more liturgically acceptable format?

That there's a hunger for such devotions I have no doubt. Call something a Novena and people attend it instinctively. There's something very appealing about a devotion that connects with the lived experience of people that is simple and quantifiable that has a continuing appeal to many people.

Whatever we may say about devotions in the past, people knew how to pray. There was a warmth, comfort and directness in our praying that seem to be missing today. While we were occasionally off beam in the past at least our hearts were in the right place. And that's probably at the core of it. Heart, not just head. Poetry, not just prose. Devotions, not just spirituality.

There are of course dangers here. An excess of devotionalism can take the faith out of religion. Obsessions with particular devotions can deflect from the centrality of the Mass. You can have too much of a good thing. But if religion becomes too spare, too pared down to the essentials, we lose the colour and warmth of the Catholic experience.

In a changing Ireland parents are now beginning to look a bit more critically at the whole question of inheritance. The last thing parents want is to have their children fighting over their inheritance. And progressively the importance of making a will and the wisdom of not disinheriting individual children are being accepted. Especially as so many are aware that the family farm could end up being divided not between siblings but between lawyers.

The price of land

If John B. Keane was alive he's probably be writing another version of *The Field*, his classic play on the Irish obsession with land. The Bull McCabe character, who killed a rival rather than let a field pass into a stranger's ownership, defines in dramatic terms that passionate intensity about land that is embedded in the Irish psyche.

But, in a changing Ireland, interest in land is taking a new turn. Once it was presumed that the son or the eldest son or the son who stayed at home would automatically inherit the family farm. Now other sons and daughters are progressively questioning this tradition. Why, in deference to tradition, should a son inherit the farm? Why not a daughter? Indeed why not an equal division for all siblings?

The question didn't arise that much in the old Ireland. Tradition was stronger. Land had less economic value. The son who stayed at home to work the farm he would eventually inherit (and to look after his parents in their old age) often got the worst side of the bargain. Sometimes 'Getting the place' was a mixed blessing, costing more than it was eventually worth.

More significantly women accepted the traditional custom of the family farm passing from father to son. But now more daughters (and sons) are looking at a track of land that could be worth a million euro and wondering why that family inheritance shouldn't be divided up. Would it not be fairer, they reasonably ask.

A daughter may have had to buy a site, to struggle to pay a mortgage and to rear her family while up the road on her family's farm a sister-in-law is driving a new 4X4, going on a few holidays a year, building an extension to the family mansion complete with conservatory and wearing designer clothes - and sitting on a few hundred acres of land from which her husband's sister has been effectively disinherited.

That's one view. Another is that the son who stayed at home may have made a huge investment in time and work and the care of ageing parents and if there is no will he will stand to inherit no more than his share. His investment of time, work, even life was made on the presumption that he would someday inherit the whole farm.

Families are complicated phenomena, allowing for a fair degree of unwarranted presumption. Sometimes parents believe that while siblings in other families fall out over the will, their children are cut from a very different cloth. But apart from the unwarranted confidence parents tend to place in the goodwill of their own children, time passes, parents die, perspectives change and sons-in-law and daughters-in-law can bring a different perspective to what 'Daddy' or 'Mammy' might have wanted. What families feel they need can become more imperative than what parents may have wanted.

Suddenly life has become very complicated. Once a girl was delighted to be 'married into' a significant farm and her husband was delighted to have another pair of hands to help out on the farm. Sometimes such practical issues didn't count because there was a haze of romance in the air and love was all that mattered. But sometimes not - apart from romance, people had a well developed sense of what constituted 'a good catch'.

Now, with marriage breakdown becoming more common, and with wives or husbands entitled to half the property, the question of land takes on a new dimension. I once heard an elderly curmudgeonly bachelor being wound up by a group of young farmers at a wedding because he hadn't married. One of the number suggested to him that he'd be better off with a bit of romance in his life. The old codger suggested that sometimes romance hadn't a lot going for it, adding,

'There isn't much romance going up the aisle of the church owning your own farm and a half an hour later coming down the aisle only owning half of it'. You mightn't sympathise with the sentiment but you can see the truth lurking behind it.

In a changing Ireland parents are now beginning to look a bit more critically at the whole question of inheritance. The last thing parents want is to have their children fighting over their inheritance. And progressively the importance of making a will and the wisdom of not disinheriting individual children are being accepted. Especially as so many are aware that the family farm could end up being divided not between siblings but between lawyers.

At the same time the hunger for land remains and the strong connection remains between a piece of ground and the generations who worked it. I once met a man who talked about the day he learned he had inherited his father's farm, the way he went straight to the farm, took off his shoes and walked around in the fields so that he could feel the grass between his toes. As if it were a religious or mystical experience which, in a certain sense, it was.

That hallowed tradition in Irish life of passing the family farm to the next generation is now on a collision course with a very different, less sentimental Ireland. The tragedy in Kilkenny – where a man bought a field, in dispute between siblings, and ended up losing his life over it – is emblematic of that new Ireland and our changing traditions. And parents are now wondering how they can ensure that they don't leave a legal and emotional mess to their children.

Changed times.

We carry restlessness around with us like a virus. And the remote control on the telly is an apt emblem. Flicking distractedly from one channel to another, watching two matches at the same time, taping a third which we know we'll never watch and listening to a commentary on another match on the radio.
Movement is a mainline drug to keep restlessness at bay.
Distraction is the background music of our lives.

Butterflies

HAVE you noticed how everyone is moving all the time now? Life today is a great sea of bustle and activity. Everyone on the move. Going to work. Bringing the children to karate. Getting to the football match. Driving the tractor. Organising the shopping,. Visiting Granny. It's not just that we seem to have so little time anymore 'to stop and stare' but that movement and activity have become a kind of drug that we need to survive.

Like when the car is in the garage getting a service. It's almost as if we experience an unease, a dislocation, because our freedom to move somewhere else is temporarily suspended. It's not that we want to go somewhere or indeed have anywhere to go but the fact that we can't move, in case we need to move, presents a greater sense of restlessness.

We bring that restlessness around with us like a virus. And the remote control on the telly is an apt emblem. Flicking distractedly from one channel to another, watching two matches at the same time, taping a third which we know we'll never watch and listening to a commentary on another match on the radio.

Or twentysomethings moving from one pub to another. Looking for something. Something better or at least different. More crack. Greater buzz. And they end up drinking the same drink, in the company of the same people, fondly imagining that because they moved through several pubs, this is really where it's at!

Or shopping. Ireland is full of people who go shopping but hardly ever, it seems to me, buy anything. I've known people who have shopped for a whole day in a shopping centre where every possible item anyone could possibly want is available in every possible size and at the end of a long day they arrive home exhausted and empty-handed. They could, they tell us, find nothing that suited them.

It isn't about shopping, of course. It's about keeping on the move and imagining that because we were able to distract and exhaust ourselves the experience had to be satisfying. Movement is a mainline drug to keep restlessness at bay. Distraction is the background music of our lives.

A friend of mine told me recently that after spending a long, empty, silent time at her father's bedside as he skirted the margins of life and death, she wondered why she found the experience so difficult. There was nowhere else in the world she wanted to be yet she felt trapped, uneasy, restless. Almost wishing she was somewhere else.

The restless spirit of our times is really about avoiding any oasis of silence or stillness or solitude because when we give ourselves time and space we begin to surface a whole range of questions: is this all my life is? what's my life for? whom do I love? who loves me? when will I die? what happens after death? is there a God? how does it all fit together? could it possibly make sense?

These are difficult questions because to get to the core of them you have to name a few unpalatable truths - about, as someone put it, 'life and death and the whole damn thing'. And that's difficult to do because the whole thrust of life is in the opposite direction: centre on your own need and satisfy it. And if ultimately you can't satisfy it, then distract yourself from it. Buying something. Or eating something. Or going somewhere.

Growing old is a good test. How do you feel about it? Do you give it much attention? Or do we begin to get uneasy when someone broaches the subject? Growing old is too close to death, the great conversation stopper. Growing old is off the agenda because the whole thrust of life today is that we have to do everything we can to arrest old age. To stay the hand of time.

Face-lifts, wrinkle-cream, buying a better car, going on an extra holiday, giving ourselves a treat, spoiling ourselves. What are they all for? What are they about? An increasingly desperate effort to deflect the reality of death, to build a protective scaffolding of pretence around ourselves?

One of the reasons religion has become unpopular is that so many have bought into a general disregard for the basic questions. Religion is seen as something negative, oppressive, backward – something that runs contrary to the spirit of our modern times when words like 'sin' and realities like 'death' have been shuffled to one side.

What we need is the time and space and silence to respect the real questions. Which is why we need significant oases of stillness and solitude to become more aware of what's ultimately important and what doesn't matter all that much. Such is the path of peace, contentment, satisfaction.

That's why we need to look again at the great wheel of activity and movement that we're turning at great cost to ourselves, moving in all directions, not allowing ourselves to sit still. Like the old story about the man who tried to capture a beautiful butterfly. The more he followed it, the more distant it was. Then exhausted he sat down and the butterfly came and rested on his shoulder.

Sport is the new religion, powered by sophisticated television presentation, the sense of identity associated with county teams and that indefinable triumph of the human spirit that finds consistent expression on the playing fields of the world. As formal religion declines and as people search for an alternative meaning in their lives, sport often seems to be the best that life can offer. And it's no coincidence that sport has taken to itself the trappings of religion and rituals.

Sport is the new religion

IS sport becoming the new religion? If ever you wanted to be convinced of that, the famous Nike advert on television is utterly convincing. It shows Portugal and Brazil getting ready for an important match. A scuffle in the tunnel leads to an impromptu kick-around. Nobody is named – nothing as obvious as that for well-informed sporting afficionados – but the line-up is impressive: Ronaldo, Ronaldino, Roberto Carlos, Luis Figo. The football control is mind-boggling, the advert must have cost a fortune to make and no one knows what it's all about until the one word 'Nike' appears at the end. In a world immersed in football, now even the advertisers don't have to say anything.

Or visit Croke Park. Especially now that the new Hill Sixteen has filled in the tooth-gap that heretofore broke the majestic sweep of the new Hogan and Cusack Stands. A triumph of modern engineering with a capacity in excess of 80,000 people, the lively new pitch, a blend of synthetic and natural grass, effortlessly becomes a swirling cauldron of noise and activity. And a part answer to a modern need. Because Croke Park, it might be said, is a new cathedral for a new faith. Because now everything, it seems – work, family, God – is becoming a backdrop to the beautiful game.

Sport is the new religion, powered by sophisticated television presentation, the sense of identity associated with county teams and even limited companies that double as premiership clubs in England and that indefinable triumph of the human spirit that finds consistent expression on the playing fields of the world.

As formal religion declines and as people search for an alternative meaning in their lives, sport often seems to be the best that life can offer. And it's no coincidence that sport has taken to itself the trappings of religion and rituals: the great cathedral of a stadium; the referee in his vestments, orchestrating the rituals like a celebrant; the umpires, altar servers in white; the linesmen as additional ministers; the hymns; and all the ancillary rituals from the entrance 'procession' to the media commentators, the sport theologians – a predictable blend of measured conservatives like John Giles and radical mavericks like Eamon Dunphy – explaining and analysing what's beyond the competence of ordinary mortals. And displacing Ss Martin (de Porres), Therese (of Liseaux) and Pio (formerly Padre) are St Ronaldo, St Thierry (Henry) and St Becks (Beckham).

That sport is the new religion can be seen from its changing relationship to the old religion. Once upon a time Sunday mornings were sacrosanct times for public worship. Now Sunday morning is a favoured sporting occasion by thousands of people who congregate for football matches, golf and a plethora of different sports. And when there's a huge clash between sport and religion on a Sunday morning religious congregations can dwindle out of sight! Regularly the new religion is seen to triumph over the old.

In other ways too sport triumphs over religion. Sport is exciting; religious worship is dismissed as boring. Religion reeks of obligation; sport is about choice, going because everyone is going, because it's the place to be – like religion used to be. Sport draws people into participation: wearing loud colours and costumes, like the leprechaun outfits in the World Cup; singing the sporting songs; waving the flags; raising the energy level; even creating an interest among those not particularly interested.

Religion seems to do the opposite. Even people who want to be at Mass often don't want to participate; you wouldn't get worshippers to dress in the liturgical equivalent of the leprechaun suit– or, if they did, they mightn't get in; they won't sing as a congregation and 99% of them refuse to join the choir; and when it comes to energy, Mass is often low wattage country with the hapless priest trying to drum up energy and interest from his own, often meagre personal resources.

In a strange way sport even promises something extra, something that connects with a deeper part of ourselves, something that has on occasion almost a mystical and spiritual meaning. In other words, what religious worship is thought to do. And, in comparison, religion seems more and more like a repetition of empty rituals that fail to connect with people's lives.

'Football', the social commentator Brian Appleyard wrote, 'is no longer a mere game, it is the great popular narrative of our time.' What has happened is that sport is not just, well, sport. Somehow the whole experience has been amplified on to a different level where it has become a kind of prism through which reality (fantasy, really) is viewed. People want to get away from a grimy, ordinary world where they are bored by repetitive work, dulled by the complexity and difficulty of relationships, reminded every waking hour of how inadequate and insipid life can be and are suckers for imagining a surrogate life where colour, significance and excitement are mediated to them through the telly in the corner of the kitchen. Once religion raised the hearts and minds. Now it's football.

The same thing is happening closer to home in the GAA world. Once it harboured in its slip-stream notions of heritage, language, faith and the Irish way of life. Now it's struggling to lose its soul with the battle almost entirely lost because of the imperative of the commercial world in which, whether it likes it or not, it has to swim to survive and grow.

It isn't football anymore. It's a mix of commerce, fantasy and religion and in a world where real religion is disappearing and where the questions life surfaces can no longer be faced it is the nearest many people get to a spiritual experience. Football is the backdrop against which everything is measured because it has succeeded in engaging the entire person. It's, to use modern cliche, the only way we know anymore to tell our story.

That's why fans wept spontaneously when Sunderland dropped out of the Premiership and wept again when they re-ascerted their place in the footballing sun. That's why perfectly lucid individuals lose the run of themselves when Mayo succeed in winning a match in the championship and imagine that one winning swallow will make for a Croke Park summer. That's part of the reason why our churches are emptying: football now carries, our hopes, our fears and our dreams.

It's easy, of course, to compare the highs of sport with the constant grind of religious ritual and worship. But the truth is that even though sport can lift the heart and mind to a higher plane and that, from time to time something mystical can happen when a performance and an occasion coalesce in sweet victory, the religious endeavour is ultimately about making contact with God. Religious worship and the rituals that underpin it may often seem boring and tedious but they are pathways to God and losing connection with them is a loss beyond words.

Funerals in Ireland are given a communal sense of importance. Neighbours give them their time. People turn out in huge numbers to offer sympathy and support. We are, as a society, at ease with the rituals of death. What happens at funeral times is that we are carried along on the prevailing current and factors like a level of faith or a commitment to things religious don't seem to matter at the time of death.

Funerals without faith

SOME years ago I was called to attend a man I did not know who had taken ill very suddenly. When I arrived the doctor was with him and he motioned me to anoint him. A friend of his then intervened and informed me that the dying man, his best friend, was 'a Protestant.'

A few days later I saw, from the death notice, that the man was in fact a Catholic. At least his remains had been taken to a Catholic Church and he had received all the rituals of Catholic burial - funeral Mass, etc - everything except anointing!

What sort of a Catholic was he, I wondered, if his best friend thought he was a Protestant? How important were his religious convictions? What did he actually believe? And when it came to his funeral arrangements did it really matter what, if anything, he believed? Would his funeral rites be any different from those of, say, Mother Teresa? Not really.

There are Catholics and Catholics in it, as we say. And nowadays a growing part of the mix of Irish life is the presence of what might be called 'cultural Catholics', people who have little or no faith, no perceptible interest in religion, no commitment, financial or otherwise, to parish. Yet, in filling in the census papers they would describe themselves as Catholics and they would be shocked if someone suggested that they shouldn't have a Christian burial. So, invariably, they get the full Catholic rituals.

Some years ago, the Humanist Association of Ireland produced a booklet entitled *Funerals without God*, a secular ceremony for those who want a non-religious funeral. I don't know how busy the Humanist Association is with secular funerals but certainly round the West of Ireland such ceremonies seem to be very thin on the ground. In rural parts, whatever about our city counterparts, we tend to bury atheists, agnostics and ambivalent 'Catholics' as if they all had a firm faith in the resurrection from the dead.

Even though the credibility of the Catholic Church has been damaged in recent years, even though religion is no longer the flavour of the month, church burials have retained their popularity.

Part of the reason is that whatever about declining congregations at weekend Masses, we live in a religious culture. For instance, the protocol of death and dying is central to people's lives, faith-ful or faith-less. We are *familiar* with it. There is an ease with the pattern: where to go, what to say, what's expected, what is not done. There is a predictability about it even to the extent that a departure like cremation - accepted by the Catholic Church - is regarded as somehow odd or eccentric.

Another factor is that the priest is central to it. An old parishioner recently bemoaned the decline in vocations: 'People are wondering' she said 'will there be a priest to bury us?' If there was no priest to baptise or to officiate at weddings, you could see people somehow working their way around it but it would be unconscionable if there was no priest there to see us off.

Another factor is the familiarity of the liturgies. The lilt of the Rosary before the coffin is closed draws us back into a familiar and comforting world in the face of grief. The solemnity of the hearse moving off from the home (or the funeral home). The shouldering of the coffin, at once a duty and a privilege, is an unspoken but moving experience. The singing of *Nearer my God to Thee* as the coffin is carried from the church somehow always seems to fit even though the words have become a bit clichéd. The holy water, the incense, the familiar prayers, the final commendation, 'Receive his soul and present him to God the most high.' And, finally, the familiar and engaging prayers at the graveside, the clay falling on the coffin, the final decade of the Rosary, all part of a ritual and a routine, at once familiar and accustomed.

Funerals in Ireland are given a communal sense of importance. Neighbours give them their time. People turn out in huge numbers to offer sympathy and support. A family, unused to the centre of the stage and broken in grief, draws comfort from the predictability of the rituals. We are, as a society, at ease with the rituals of death. What happens at funeral times is that we are carried along on the prevailing current and factors like a level of faith or a commitment to things religious don't seem to matter at the time of death.

I find this in myself. I find it dispiriting to baptise a child where no one in the congregation seems the least bit interested in the religious dimension. It is equally dispiriting to officiate at a wedding which would have been in a civil registry office if social parental expectations and the possibility of better photographs for the wedding album hadn't won the argument for the church. Yet I find that funerals of people with little or no faith, no perceptible interest during their lives in God or religion, are still significant faith experiences. Maybe it is that death and the rituals that attend it are so stark and elemental that every funeral is in some sense a rehearsal for one's own. Or maybe it is that when death comes we all revert to an instinctive belief in the hereafter! Either way, Baptism or marriage in church may become less popular but in death no one really knows what else to do except what we've always done.

Without context we end up on a merry-go-round of activity and movement that never seems to get us to where we want to be. Without context we end up living and working for the future, forgetting the present and letting the happiness of the present moment slip through our fingers. How many of us will, in future years, look back on the lives we live now and realise that these are actually the great days that in years to come we will look on with great fondness?

Why have you stopped praying?

It's a cheeky question to ask, I know. Because, like the question, *Have you stopped beating your wife?* it makes all kinds of presumptions. Not least that people don't pray. Or that prayer has any value. Or that there's a consensus on how we define what 'prayer' is, which of course there isn't. One man's meat . . . and so forth.

But what I'm trying to get at, I suppose, is the way that society has changed, the way we've all changed. The sense that something peculiar has been going on and suddenly we come round a bend in life and there it is staring us in the face. Like coming to a clearance in the middle of a great forest.

Part of what has happened, I think, is that the religious enterprise has been sidelined in Irish life. And just as, in the past, we went along with the crowd going to weekend Mass, now we find ourselves, almost indiscernably, making a u-turn and following the crowd going in the opposite direction.

It has something to do with time. Once we had no labour-saving devices and yet we had plenty of time. Now everything we use saves time but we seem to end up with less of it than we ever had. We have become part of a bustling world where time, time for ourselves, time for our families, quality time has disappeared.

With less time comes less space. Less room for attending to ourselves and the questions that try to surface in our lives: what is my life for? what does it all mean? where does God fit in? how can I put some shape on the twists and turns of my life?

And with less time and space comes less context. Because without time and space it's not possible to stand back and see the subtle patterns in the tapestries our lives weave. Without context we can end up imagining that we know it all, that what is past has no value, that maturity and wisdom can come from the pages of a book or the advice of a guru rather than out of the distilled wisdom of a lived life.

Without context we end up on a merry-go-round of activity and movement that never seems to get us to where we want to be. Without context we end up living and working for the future, forgetting the present and letting the happiness of the present moment slip through our fingers. Even though we all know that waiting to live is a fool's charter. Love, the poet Seamus Heaney, said somewhere, love the life you're shown.

How many parents, for example, are trying to survive their children's childhood rather than enjoying, even savouring those short magical years? How many parents imagine that beyond the frustrations of the teenage years there is some Nirvana without worry or unreason? How many people on their death-beds regret that they didn't spend more time at work and less time with their families? How many of us will, in future years, look back on the lives we live now and realise that these are actually the great days that in years to come we will look on with great fondness? How many of us live as if beyond the limitations of our present lives, there is a tranquil sea that we will live forever to enjoy?

There isn't. There's just death. And that's the ultimate context. Life, no matter how long, is always limited. There is a point beyond which none of us will go. And there is a wisdom that comes from holding that reference point in our heads, not in any morose way but as a way of distinguishing the important from the peripheral.

Giving ourselves time and space and context is, I believe, ultimately about giving ourselves a context for prayer. It's about welcoming the essential questions scrambling for attention just under the surface of our lives. It's about facilitating a religious quest that can enrich the lives we live now.

Hands up all those who believe that our recent prosperity, great as it is, has made us any happier as individuals, families or society. Why then do we allow the quest for more to colonise large portions of our lives and to leave us scraping around for time and space to feed the relationships that are the bread and butter of human fulfilment? How many spouses will one day see clearly the potential for happiness in a relationship that they now take for granted? How many former children will stand at a parent's grave, overwhelmed with love and appreciation for a dead father or mother and who will spend the rest of their lives trying to forgive themselves for not seeing before what's so obvious now? Why is it that we have to live so long before we learn so little? Why is it that we can only appreciate what we have when we experience its absence?

We know it all now, of course. The past is a distant country. We've nothing to learn now. So we get caught pushing life to its limits because we imagine that the more we get or eat or own or enjoy, the happier we will be. And then when something happens, someone is seriously ill or a loved one is dead, and we find ourselves kneeling in the back seat of some church, asking a God we scarcely believe in to come to the rescue of a life that ignores his presence. Something within us resonates with the beyond but we've forgotten the words.

So to get back to my question: why have you stopped praying?

Some parents have bought the pop psychology pedalled in recent years by any number of (mainly) American gurus, the basic premise of which is that parents should be popular with their children.
'My Mum is my best friend' sort of gibberish.
Parents are not supposed to be best friends with their children.
They are supposed to be parents.

Teenage Sex

IF the morning-after pill for sexually-active eleven year-olds is the answer, as Mary Harney seemed to suggest some time back, then I'm afraid we'll have to look for a different question. Because, apart from anything else, that approach is taking the focus and the responsibility off parents and placing it exactly where it shouldn't be - on THEM, on whatever convenient scapegoat parents use to deflect their responsibility - on the government, the social services, the medical system or whoever. Isn't it a convenient time for parents to be reminded that they are supposed to be, well, parents?

In fairness to Harney, she has injected a much-needed realism into a difficult area. We're now a long, long way from de Valera's maidens dancing at the crossroads. Or even the showband era when the *Clipper Carlton* and *The Royal* were in their prime. Or even the discos of the 90s when a certain restraint was still in order.

Now with the increasing sexual explicitness of television programmes, the easy availability of soft pornography on magazines stands and on extra-terrestrial television, the consequent growing sexualization of young people and the sundering of traditional boundaries, within the space of a decade or more we have been catapulted from an enclosed and insular way of life into an international culture where choice is the optimum consideration. This rapid transformation has even affected our language: modesty is now just a synonym for humility.

One result of all this is that many parents who grew up in a different world can't cope with and don't want to hear about the realities of life today for their children. Some of the facts are as follows. Young teens regularly attend discos in skimpy clothes they bring in a hold-all and change into in the toilet. On and off the dance floor, they cross boundaries in a manner that would make their parents blush. And the bravado world that young teens inhabit and the expectations they inflict on each other bounce them into a level of sexual activity that often they don't want or at least don't really feel all that comfortable with.

Probably, the most telling truth of all is that parents often have an unreasonable level of confidence in their own children. My John or my Emma wouldn't behave like that! They do, they do. Because, let's be honest, if you hadn't the limitations when you were their age - sexy clothes, money, travel and out on the town at thirteen - how do you think you'd behave?

Especially if, as used to be the case a few years back, your neighbour (probably a friend of your parents) was keeping an eye out at the back of the hall. Or a few years before that the PP was standing with his arms folded and a beady eye on the proceedings. Now discos often seem to be run by Twentysomethings out to make their first million and who cares about a neighbour's child?

The first problem with the growing sexualisation of children and the sexual activity it generates is to get parents to recognise what's happening. The second is to get parents to act as parents.

The problem that Mary Harney tried to solve by suggesting that the morning after pill might need to be available to 11 year-old girls is fundamentally about parenting, bad parenting. As Brenda Power pointed out in a column in *The Sunday Tribune*, if girls of 11 years of age are sexually active and in danger of becoming pregnant, it means that parents are neglectful and irresponsible.

11 year-olds are not young adults; they are not even teenagers; they're children. And children need to be cared for, supervised, directed and, more particularly, not allowed to establish little

independent republics in their own homes where they can decide when, where, what and with whom they will do anything they want.

We need, I think, to keep things in perspective here. There are thousands and thousands of young kids who are not sexually active: because (i) they heed their parents; or (ii) they are not prepared to bend to peer pressure; or (iii) they are clued in enough to realise that they are neither physically or psychologically ready for a full physical relationship, least of all for giving birth to and caring for a baby; or (iv) their parents will ensure, in so far as its possible, that the circumstances will not exist to encourage it – no sleeping over, no drink, no unsupervised discos, no late nights, no making adult decisions when they're hardly out of nappies.

One problem is that some parents have lost their nerve and have allowed their children to run rings around them. First by convincing them that legitimate parental control and responsibility are out of sync with the brave new world of today and that moral values have suddenly become old-fashioned. Another problem is that some parents have bought the pop psychology pedalled in recent years by any number of (mainly) American gurus, the basic premise of which is that parents should be popular with their children. 'My Mum is my best friend' sort of gibberish.

Parents are not supposed to be best friends with their children. They are supposed to be parents. And sometimes that means saying *No*. Sometimes that means saying hard things out of sheer love. Real love. Not the folksy sort of nonsense that disappears with the morning dew. If parents were parents Mary Harney wouldn't be trying to take us up yet another side road.

> *What seems to be happening is that a new coarseness, an insidious vulgarity is creeping over life in the form of a mock modernity or sophistication and people have come to accept it as part of the price they have to pay for living in the modern world. Why that is so is difficult to imagine. After all is there anything more pathetic than listening to someone peppering his or her conversation with expletives in the belief that they are impressing someone, anyone.*

A limited vocabulary

I watched the comedian, Tommy Tiernan, on *The Late Late Show* recently with the sound turned down. The last time he was on *The Late Late* was during Gay Byrne's time and Tiernan's mix of coarseness, bad language and to my untutored mind, unfunny material seemed on the wrong side of pathetic. But apparently, his performance did the trick. He became famous or at least noticed because by infamously lowering standards and insulting a raft of people, he provoked a reaction. And, I'm told, for people who like that kind of thing, he became something of a hero.

This time when Tommy Tiernan appeared on my screen with a gushing Pat Kenny - what happens to Kenny when he moves from radio to television? - I decided to avoid a repeat of the same. So instead I turned down the sound and read a chapter of a book.

A bad decision because apparently Tiernan was even more 'controversial' than the last time and spent a lot of his time saying outrageous things about priests and the Catholic Church as well as peppering the airwaves with expletives, a strategy always guaranteed to win brownie points among a certain audience. So I missed it and am not in a position to comment on it. Bad decision.

A few weeks later there was outrage in Holland because a film-maker, who did a documentary on violence in Muslim marriages, was killed by an outraged Muslim as he cycled to work. It raises the question about how acceptable it would be, even in Ireland, to excoriate the Muslim faith or Muslim clergy. Will some outraged Catholic in a balaclava be found hunting for Tommy Tiernan in Navan or thereabouts. Probably not. And just as well. It could make his career.

But then I said to myself, here's a young guy on the make, trying to make a name for himself and reacting to the expectations of his typical audience. And, after all, RTE made an apology of sorts when the expected reaction to Tiernan's performance was greater than they had anticipated. So, move on. Get a life. The sky hasn't fallen in.

But part of the sky did fall in a few days later when Terry Prone was commenting on the American election on local radio and used a vulgarity as part of her stream of conversation. Did she have to? Did she notice? And on the same day *The Star* newspaper reached an all-time low in a front-page headline that famously used another vulgarity. Yes, I know the old *Star* is hardly the *Times Literary Supplement*, but you begin to wonder whether we will all eventually drown in a sea of coarseness and vulgarity.

It could be that we're just growing old. Or that people give up fighting the same fight all the time. But should we not protest that the level of coarseness in our society is getting out of hand? Once people used bad language because they lacked the vocabulary to express themselves and they ended up using the one adjective over and over again. Or people used bad language, as children sometimes do, to show-off, to get attention, to demand that people notice them. Or people occasionally lost it and ended up cursing and blaspheming and whatever you're having yourself. But now bad language seems no more than an extension of the general vocabulary. It's everywhere now. Everywhere you go it's like a demented Greek chorus, F-this and F-that and F-the other.

What seems to be happening is that a new coarseness, an insidious vulgarity is creeping over life in the form of a mock modernity or sophistication and people have come to accept it as part of the price they have to pay for living in the modern world. Why that is so is difficult to imagine. After all is there anything more pathetic than listening to someone peppering his or her conversation with expletives in the belief that they are impressing someone, anyone.

As in other areas the key principle is respect. Clive James once defined blasphemy as a form of ultimate disrespect for someone's religious principles. And coarseness and bad language are ultimately a form of disrespect for other people. And for the person using them if they had the nous to understand it.

But what do you do? I often feel like stopping someone in mid-sentence and saying to them that I feel insulted and disrespected by their language. It's not just that you can imagine the response. Or that you allow yourself to be presented as precious and prissy. It's just that people don't actually notice it anymore. F-this and F-that and so forth have become part of general use.

Yet if you don't say anything, you find that you get carried along on this sea of coarseness and you find yourself accepting that it doesn't really matter anymore. That language changes. That vocabularies expand. That what was unacceptable in one generation becomes acceptable in another. That nobody cares.

But I care. And I know others care. And if I have no problem saying that I'm not happy for people to invade my space with tobacco smoke, why should I have any problem objecting to my space being invaded by some idiot mouthing expletives?

On the other hand, maybe it's just the onset of old age.

At the end of the interview Dorgan asked Ahern if he was disappointed at the sleaze unearthed by the tribunals. Ahern concurred and then remarked that what he found hard to understand was why, when people had enough, they still wanted more. It seemed to genuinely puzzle him and he mulled over it as if he was trying to work out a complicated bit of trigonometry.

Ambivalent legacy

On Lyric FM, the poet Theo Dorgan, interviewed An Taoiseach, Bertie Ahern. Apparently it's part of the recent media effort to create a bit of momentum in the run-up to the general election. For that reason too, presumably, Bertie even submitted himself to the ordeal of spending a number of days in the company of flaky Hector, once of TG4 and, amazingly, lived to tell the tale.

But back to the more civilised world of Lyric FM. At the end of the interview Dorgan asked Ahern if he was disappointed at the sleaze unearthed by the tribunals. Ahern concurred and then remarked that what he found hard to understand was why, when people had enough, they still wanted more. It seemed to genuinely puzzle him and he mulled over it as if he was trying to work out a complicated bit of trigonometry.

I have no doubt but that Ahern is a good man. Decent. Genuine. Hard-working. Fair. A bit old-fashioned. You could imagine him togging out at the side of a Gaelic football field in the Fifties. Or standing at the back of a Ballroom of Romance saying 'How'ya' to everyone that passed him by. A bit out of sync maybe with the new Ireland he helped to create. Possibly becoming a bit reflective as he ponders the ambivalent legacy of the Celtic Tiger. And wondering perhaps when the sums are added up whether what we have become is more or less than what we were.

This is more, I think, than a sentimental attachment to the way we were. I think Ahern and many more experience a sadness that the new Ireland seems less than the sum of its parts. We have money, certainly. A prosperity undreamt of by past generations. And jobs. And cars. And holidays in the sun. And lovely homes. On the pig's back, the old people would have called it. And God knows it has more going for it than poverty and unemployment and no transport except the old bicycle and no running water in the house.

But there's a new greed in the air, what Bertie Ahern referred to in that interview, and why in a writer in the *Irish Times* defined modern Ireland as: "Forty Shades of Greed." We have enough but we want more. More money for less work. A second or even a third car. Two holidays. Two homes. Less tax. And if you can't hack it then it's your own fault if you go to the wall. Natural selection. Market forces, they call it. The triumph of the fittest. If you can't prosper in the new prosperity then it's too bad.

Once we believed that if Ireland grew prosperous overnight we wouldn't lose the run of ourselves. We knew enough about want to know that there was a communal responsibility to look after those not able to look after themselves. When a bread-winner died neighbours saved the hay or, equivalently, looked after things. It was, we always felt, the least we might do. A helping hand in time of need was part of the vocabulary of our lives. And if the good days ever arrived we'd spread it around a bit because it was only right. If there was solidarity and community in the bad times we'd use the same currency if we got rich. Or so we thought.

We imagined we were better than we are. Now a new selfishness stalks the land. Now the unemployed are reviled because there are jobs for everyone - even though everyone knows that long-term unemployment is a complex social reality. Get out there on your bike and get one, as Maggie Thatcher's ministers used to say. Now those who argue for the rights of the poor are despised as do-gooders, at odds with the new Thatcherite wisdom. Now those whose boats weren't lifted by the tide of the new buoyant Irish economy are shuffled to the sidelines, even if they had no boats at all.

But it's not just the new selfishness. It's also a new corrosiveness of respect and dignity. Excess is all. It isn't enough to have a good time, you have to get drunk first before you can enjoy it. It isn't enough to get high on life you have to supplement the excitement with drugs. Excess has become endemic in present society.

Stand at a street corner at two o'clock in the morning and watch the luckiest, the most molly-coddled and the best educated generation of young Ireland. See the young men falling around the place and young women falling out of their dresses. Listen to their conversation, peppered with expletives and blasphemies, and ask yourself whether we should be proud of them. Read about gurriers attacking an immigrant for no better reason than that he has a dark skin and think of the abuse dished out to Irish emigrants in other countries in the past and cringe with embarrassment that we are now doing to others what we ourselves experienced in the past.

In the old days poverty was regarded as an unacceptable excuse for lack of respect for ourselves or for others. Nowadays prosperity and excess seem to justify the lowest of personal and social standards.

Once, in what we believed were the bad old days, we were able to deal with poverty. I'm not too sure that, in the good times, we can do the same with prosperity.

It is a common experience nowadays to meet people who have more money than they know what to do with, more material possessions than they ever dreamed about, more answers to questions that they thought could never be explained and yet there's something missing - some important constituent of life that they can't get a handle on. And they experience a hunger deep within themselves that nothing seems to satisfy.

Hungers of the heart

THERE used to be a wisdom about the decline of religion. One day when science explained all the mysteries of the world and when everyone was well off, we'd no longer need God. As adults of a brave new world one day we'd look back on the naive, unsophisticated and superstitious nonsense we called religion and wonder how we could have been so deluded. Then we'd know that religion was at best, a fiction, and at worst, a conspiracy to keep people under control. Then we'd know that religion was the opium of the people. Then we'd know that God was dead.

But now religion and science are forging a new respect for one another. Now people with successful careers, plenty of money, a superfluity of material possessions are beginning to ask, Is this all there is? Why is it that so many with so much want something more? In our brave new world, when every appetite can be satisfied and every need filled, why is the itch still there?

It is a common experience nowadays to meet people who have more money than they know what to do with, more material possessions than they ever dreamed about, more answers to questions that they thought could never be explained and yet there's something missing – some important constituent of life that they can't get a handle on. And they experience a hunger deep within themselves that nothing seems to satisfy. The simple truth is that there is in everyone, in some shape or form, a hunger for meaning, for spirituality, ultimately for God, that is just below the surface of life and that seeks, even demands some kind of confirmation.

The great philosopher, Blaise Pascal, said that in everyone there is an abyss that only God can fill. St Augustine wrote about our hearts being restless until they rest in God. It is a common experience. There is an itch of restlessness that can only be contained by experiencing a life-sustaining spirituality and a reflectiveness that provides a context for mulling over the great and the small issues of a lived life.

These thoughts are occasioned by two recent experiences. One was a chat with a highly intelligent, very successful man in his early thirties who has decided to leave behind a very promising journalistic and academic career and to go into a monastery. He has plenty of money, friends, fulfilling work but he wants more and he's going to trust in God and throw himself in at the deep end. That, in a sense is the honours course.

The pass course is represented by a friend of mine who told me recently that as he gets older – he's in his thirties too – he feels more and more the need for an opportunity to focus on the spiritual side of life. He wants an opportunity to reflect, to pray, to worship in ways that are personally satisfying to him. He finds Mass on Sunday in his local church a rushed and frustrating experience. People are jammed into seats, there's little opportunity for silence, often there's no choir, the sermon is unprepared and unconvincing at a number of levels, everyone seems to be – like hounds in a trap – waiting to get away. There is, he says, a space in his life, a hunger in his heart that he wants to fill but he can't find an agreeable and satisfying way to do it.

Sometimes, I think, that as the numbers going to Mass decrease – as the disinterested and the uncommitted fall away and there is less social pressure to conform – there will be a variety of very different needs to be met from different groups of people. Instead of or alongside the main Sunday Mass, at which the local community will worship as community, maybe people will begin to opt for a number of alternative liturgies.

It could well be that a small group of people, say less than 20, would gather one evening a week for a quiet and reflective Eucharist. The focus would be on providing a place where the readings would be read slowly, their meaning teased out, the sermon a group discussion on the theme of the Mass, the bidding prayers individual responses to how readings impinge on the lived experiences of the group, a lot of silence, gentle music, quiet lighting from candles to create an ambiance of acceptance and calm.

I have no doubt but that there are thousands of people who would love that kind of intimate and personal liturgy that would provide a creative and deeply satisfying space in the hectic lives we lead. Just as people now attend the most esoteric, self-improvement courses - on everything from karate to creative embroidery - there is a crying need for a place and a space that would help to satisfy the hungers of our hearts, our minds, our souls.

Since the new procedures were introduced and the first crop of newly-ordained women came on stream appointments to the most prestigious parishes have been dominated by attractive, vibrant young women, gushing with self-confidence, bubbling with personality and oozing with empathy.

A vacancy in Abbeylaffy

IT'S the year 2050 a.d. in the Parish of Abbeylaffy and the PP, Very Rev. Noreen Treacy, having reached the mandatory retirement age of 65, has just retired. Consequently, there's a vacancy for a new PP and soon the process of appointment will be initiated as the usual procedures are put in place: parish assembly to prioritise parish needs, discussion at parish council level, job specification, advertisements, interviews, recommendations, approval of bishop and eventual appointment.

When Noreen was appointed PP in Abbeylaffy way back in 2024 it was under the old appointments procedure. The bishop looked into his heart and decided that Canon (as she then was) Noreen should be offered the position. (The Chapter of Canons has since been abolished.) In the old days, when a PP was appointed there was no discussion with the people, no consultation with the Parish Council, no interview for the position. It seems remarkable by today's standards but that was the way it was then. A bit of history to put things in context. At the turn of the century, the reforms of the Second Vatican Council had not been fully implemented. Some parishes didn't even have Parish Councils or Parish Finance committees, even though they were required in the law of the Catholic Church.

Then Pope John the Twenty-Fourth, the successor of Pope Benedict XVI, in an effort to kick-start reform, delivered his famous ultimatum, in his encyclical *Fuimus (We have had our day)* to the entire Catholic church. *Fuimus* gave each bishop two years, under penalty to interdict, to introduce what came to be known as the Lateran Reforms. In parishes failing to implement the reforms, the faithful, while remaining in communion with the church, were told they would be denied the sacraments and priests, guilty of blocking the reforms, were threatened with suspension. And in dioceses failing to meet the Papal deadline, bishops were told they would be summarily retired. (Remarkably, the reforms went through without a hitch, and on time.)

Then John XXIV's successor, Paul VII, grasped the nettle of women's ordination in his celebrated encyclical *Fiat justitia (Let justice be done)* and procedures and structures for appointing PPs stemmed from the flood of activity generated by the burst of energy and vitality that followed. By virtue of their baptism (and their collections) it came to be seen as an issue of justice that parishioners would have a say in the appointment of their PP - thus, the parish assembly, guided by a trained facilitator, where parish needs are discussed and everyone can have their say. Then the discussion at parish council where the precise job specification for prospective candidates is finalised.

Then the placing of advertisements in local and national media; the appointment of a selection board; the interviews with the selected candidates; the recommendation of the selection board; the approval of the parish council; and finally the approval of the bishop.

In the case of Abbeylaffy, the initial consultation with the people in the parish assembly surfaced a number of obvious needs. While Rev. Noreen's extended tenure as PP was successful in many respects, it was felt that the new PP should have a wider range of abilities and interests and the assembly recommended to the selection board a series of questions that should be asked of prospective candidates. Among them were: What priority should be given to the participation of the people in the decisions of the parish? In previous parishes what was the record of the candidate with youth, liturgy, home visitation, inter-church activities, choirs etc.? Can he/she sing? What are his/her professional qualifications? Is he/she prepared to participate in Abbeylaffy's very successful emigrant reunions? Will he/she be prepared to continue and develop the involvement of people in the running of the parish? Is he/she personable and easy to get on with? Has he/she any vocational idiosyncrasies? Were there any difficulties in his/her previous appointments? What was his/her work ethic like? Can he/she preach?

In the event, the assembly strongly indicated that, while it was in no way a comment on Noreen's gender or her long and successful tenure as PP, a younger man be appointed on this occasion, 'younger' in this instance meaning someone under 60.

The adverts have been placed in the media as specified in the procedures and, as Abbeylaffy is regarded as something of a plum in priestly circles, it is expected that a number of promising candidates will apply. Since the new procedures were introduced and the first crop of newly-ordained women came on stream appointments to the most prestigious parishes have been dominated by attractive, vibrant young women, gushing with self-confidence, bubbling with personality and oozing with empathy.

As a result, seminaries, closed down in the later stages of the last century, are now reopening; parishes, amalgamated in the early decades when the number of male-only ordinations had practically ceased, are now thriving; deacons, introduced in 2008 to offset the decline in ordinations, are almost extinct; and Confessions, almost non-existent in the latter days of John Paul II's pontificate, have increased significantly.

One issue not addressed by the parish assembly was the condition of the Parochial House which has fallen into some disrepair. (Noreen let things slip a bit on the domestic front in her declining years). What will happen, someone asked, if the best candidate is a married priest with a young family? (The requirement of celibacy was set aside in 2015.) Will his wife or her husband or partner be turned off the appointment when she/he sees the condition of the house? Eventually it was agreed that the refurbishment of the house be set aside until it became clear whether the new PP was married or had a family. Plans to modernise the house with en-suite bedrooms, the addition of a conservatory to the east-wing and a nursery have been placed on hold.

Interviews are expected to take place within four weeks.

How many sermons can you actually remember? Of the thousands of sermons you've heard in the thousands of Masses you've attended, how many do you actually remember. Ann Wroe, who writes a regular column in The Tablet, says that she only remembers two: one on the subject of miniskirts (he wasn't in favour of them) and the other at school when she was distracted by the gaunt beauty of the Jesuit who delivered it. Not a great repertoire after a lifetime of Mass attendance.

A man speaking

THE Anglican priest and poet R.S. Thomas wrote somewhere that there are more secrets waiting to be told when we are older and can stand the truth. A friend of mine offers his tuppenceworth about sermons. There's one way, he says, to solve the problem about sermons once and for all. Do away with them. Give them up. Not just for Lent but forever. Forget about them. And at one fell swoop, you will brighten up both the clergy's Saturdays and the laity's Sundays.

There's something about a cool, crisp solution that appeals to us. And maybe this is it. After all, sermons are generally terrible. I shouldn't say that of course. Letting the side down and all that. Being a practitioner of sorts. But it's true, isn't it? Once you say "This is the Gospel of The Lord" you can see the collective glaze descend on the congregation, as in a dentist's waiting room when people pour over uninteresting magazines and nod to each other in feigned interest. Everything about the posture, body language and demeanour suggests that the assembled faithful want you to get on with it. Make it as painless as possible.

Some say that sermons used to be good. That's another myth. The truth probably is that in the past they were probably even worse than they are now. Because the Mass was in Latin and we spent the time parroting impregnable phrases from a foreign language and trying to distract ourselves from the tedium, the priest breaking into English was something of a change. At least you could understand the words. Or most of them.

Nor is it true that years ago there were great preachers like Bishop Fulton Sheen, Fr Patrick Peyton and the anti-poteen Redemptorist, Fr Conneally and that we don't have any great preachers anymore. Sheen and Peyton and Conneally, like de Valera and John Dillon, were an acquired taste. To see that just look back at some of the film clips of the time and you wonder where the great reputations came from.

The truth is that Sheen and Peyton, like de Valera and Dillon, were different rather than memorable. What mattered was not what they said but the fact that they said it. The reputation preceded the talking. And without the reputation, the sermons and what passed for political oratory seemed thin enough gruel in retrospective.

After all, how many sermons can you actually remember? Of the thousands of sermons you've heard in the thousands of Masses you've attended, how many do you actually remember. Ann Wroe, who writes a regular column in *The Tablet*, says that she only remembers two: one on the subject of miniskirts (he wasn't in favour of them) and the other at school when she was distracted by the gaunt beauty of the Jesuit who delivered it. Not a great repertoire after a lifetime of Mass attendance.

The problem with the sermon is that it is impossible to achieve. We're into conflicting expectations here. Black or white or grey? Explaining the readings in tortuous detail or opening a shaft of light in the darkness? Dressing down the world or celebrating faith? Rubbing people down or putting them through the wringer? Or, like a stray dog, going a bit of the road with everyone?

Some want you to preach the Ten Commandments. Others want you to give some indication that you have a sense of how complex moral decisions can be. Some want you to lay down the law (usually for someone else). Others feel the need for a bit of encouragement, a sense that the preacher understands or better still sympathises with the compulsions of their lives. And the more you answer one need, the less you defer to the other needs.

Another part of the problem is that to communicate well you have to share part of yourself. The sermons that people remember are when the person gets out from behind the priest and a human being reveals himself to us. I once heard a priest talk about how difficult he finds it to say Mass, that he sometimes wonders what he believes and that all of his life was a pilgrim path around and through periods of great doubt. You could sense the interest in the congregation. The words were uncertain, the constructions left a lot to be desired, in football terms he was more often in the *Vauxhall Conference* than in the Premiership but what people heard was a man speaking.

Priests aren't good at this. Anyway it's hard to do it fifty-two Sundays a year (with a few holydays thrown in) and, in these inquisitive times, have a bit of your life left for yourself. But at least we know how it works. You have to press the right buttons so that people at least know that you can see the right questions even if you're not sure of all the answers.

So should we give up the sermons altogether or struggle on? Can we find a middle way between the *Weighty Words About Life* and *Random Thoughts While Shaving*? Suggestions on a postcard please. But don't send them to me. Find somewhere closer to home.

The presenting reason for the document was the need to respond to a perception that there is a growing, disproportionate number of homosexual priests and seminarians. The reasoning is that there should be a balance between heterosexual and homosexual in the priesthood, a balance broadly based on the general population. This is a dodgy point for the Vatican because the same argument can be made for women priests.

Unwise words

Bishop Willie Walsh was right when he said that the recent Vatican document on homosexuality and the priesthood came at a bad time for the Irish Church. Given, he said, 'the dark winter of the Church in Ireland' the timing was unhelpful. He was also critical of its starkness. It would have been better, he said, if it had appeared in a broader context, like canvassing vocations to the priesthood. Few, I think, would disagree with those opinions.

A further consideration might be whether, in the long run, this document will be more trouble than it's worth for the Catholic Church. Because in a sense, it is saying nothing new. Anything it says about homosexual priests or seminarians could also be said about their heterosexual equivalents. The general gist of the document – men who practised homosexuality or presented deep-seated homosexual tendencies or supported the so-called gay culture couldn't be ordained as priests – applies equally to heterosexuals. As does the statement that those with temporary homosexual tendencies must have overcome them for three years before they can be ordained. A similar statement could be made in reference to heterosexuals: those who are heterosexually active or those with obsessive heterosexual tendencies or those who supported the macho heterosexual culture . . .

So why the document at all? The presenting reason for the document was the need to respond to a perception that there is a growing, disproportionate number of homosexual priests and seminarians. The reasoning is that there should be a balance between heterosexual and homosexual in the priesthood, a balance broadly based on the general population. This is a dodgy point for the Vatican because the same argument can be made for women priests. If half the population is excluded from priesthood, what about that particular imbalance? If the membership of priesthood should reflect the general population how come half the population (i.e. women) are not represented at all? And why get uptight about the growing numbers of homosexual priests, if no one is getting similarly excited about no women in the priesthood?

One of the prices to be paid for surfacing this issue is that it will serve to alienate priests and seminarians who are homosexual. While the document doesn't say that homosexuals can't become priests, and it doesn't say that homosexuals who are priests are any less priests than heterosexuals, the bluntness of the language must make gay priests feel distinctly uncomfortable, if not inadequate. Even though gay priests bring to priesthood a gentleness and sensitivity often missing from their heterosexual colleagues, the feeling that they are somehow being tolerated rather than cherished may have lasting repercussions for them.

The document too, I think, will serve to further alienate the wider gay community. As a Church we find it difficult to express our teaching on homosexuality without it being perceived as insulting, dismissive, judgemental. While in theory for church spokespersons the categories may seem clear, when you actually talk to gay Catholics struggling to make sense of their sexuality when it intersects with their religion, the reality seems quite different. What they perceive as condemnation from the Church of Jesus Christ can't be squared with the compassion and love of their Lord and Saviour. I wonder how many of those who wrote the recent document on homosexuality and priesthood actually talked to homosexual priests about it.

Certainly the document will seriously discommode homosexual Catholics who are clinging to the edges of Church, another finger prised off the edge.

I recently over-heard at Mass an elderly priest condemning gay marriage. It was in relation to a recent legal case challenging the status quo about marriage. The priest, full of himself, talked in a disparaging, condemnatory tone about gays and sneered at their attempts to establish permanent unions. As he spoke I wondered what the gays in his congregation must be feeling. How did they feel, I wondered, being portrayed as some kind of diseased under-class rather than as human beings loved by God and maybe struggling to make sense of an orientation that was not of their choosing. And could anyone blame them if they never set foot in that church again? Or how parents of a homosexual must have felt to hear their own flesh and blood being disowned, in effect, by their own church? And as the priest ranted on, he seemed to have no idea at all of the damage he was doing as he trampled all over people.

My fear would be that there's going to be a lot of collateral damage from this document. What presented as an effort to achieve a better balance in the Church between homosexual and heterosexual priests could become a divisive and debilitating force as a Church that strives to communicate with a changing world finds itself unable to find the right words. It may also damage the authority of the Church in today's world because it feeds the perception that the Church is out of touch.

My own feeling is that in future years we will conclude that this particular document simply wasn't worth it: it will be impossible to apply; the Church may well regret the confusion in the document between homosexuality and paedophilia; and, unnervingly, bishops in America are publicly confronting each other about its content, progressives interpreting it in a liberal way and traditionalists in a conservative way.

While the document seeks to draw a line that suggests we're at the end of something, it may well be that, in years to come, we will see the publication of this document as a beginning rather than an ending.

The Catholic Church may be the recipient of a great deal of anger and hostility but it is also the crucible of a culture, a ritual and a tradition that mediate to us not just the accumulated wisdom of the past but a sense of the beauty and the vitality at the heart of life.

The Catholic experience

Not too many people know this, as the actor Michael Caine might say, but the word is that Shakespeare was a Catholic. Scholars are now tentatively moving in the direction of saying that it was the wellspring of Catholic faith and learning that fuelled his genius. That bit of news won't set the hearts pounding – for a number of reasons. For most people Shakespeare will forever be associated with impenetrable gobbledegook that they had to wade through for the Leaving Certificate. For others, we have moved on from the excitement of President Kennedy's and Princess Grace's Catholicism. The word *Catholic*, once a badge of pride and honour, now has to be used more carefully. The provocative Catholicism of yesteryear is now somewhat more muted.

We live in changed times and I don't have to rehearse the point here. Now, for some, *Catholic* is almost a negative word. In the thesaurus of our times it has become synonymous with control, oppression, even betrayal. And part of the fall-out from the times we live in is that fewer people feel comfortable with the word *Catholic*, more people are drifting away from the public practice of their Catholic faith and a space is opening in Irish life between Catholicism and what really matters in Irish life.

The danger now is that we might throw the baby out with the bathwater. Anger at the Catholic Church for its perceived betrayals of trust, resentment at its control in areas like education or health, discomfort in declaring an allegiance to its policies can lead to a gradual jettisoning of the great Catholic heritage that is the birthright of so many of our people. John O'Donohue, the poet and philosopher, recently appealed to people who had walked away from the Catholic Church, not to walk away from their Catholic culture and heritage.

What people sometimes forget is that the Catholic heritage is greater and wider and richer than the Catholic Church. Stand among the ruins of Clonmacnoise, or for that matter Moyne and Rosserk, and is it possible not to sense that somehow that ruined world resonates with a bit of us somewhere deep within? Read the Fathers of the Church and is it possible not to feel that somehow out of that distant world there is the promise of making sense of the tantalisingly complex world we live in today. Attend a funeral and let the rituals of death unfold as the quiet dignity and solemnity of the occasion carries a message that hangs in the air as surely as the smell of incense fills the church? Take time to look at the beautiful Evie Hone stain-glass window in Tirrane Church in the Mullet and let the beauty enter your soul.

The Catholic Church may be the recipient of a great deal of anger and hostility but it is also the crucible of a culture, a ritual and a tradition that mediate to us not just the accumulated wisdom of the past but a sense of the beauty and the vitality at the heart of life.

For some Catholics their experience of Church is of a narrowness that discomforts and repels. For others there is a largeness of vision that draws them into a lived experience of healing, forgiveness and reconciliation. For some all that seems to matter by way of Catholic teaching is abortion. For others there is a breadth of inclusiveness that places a wider focus on the larger issues of global poverty and local injustice. For some Catholicism is a huge ship, isolated and triumphal and authoritative, on a huge tranquil ocean. For others it is a small craft picking its way on a choppy sea.

It isn't the old refrain of *Once a Catholic, always a Catholic*. Rather it is that in the lives we lead, the Catholic thing is inextricably tied with the way we function as human beings. Some couples now marry in the

Catholic Church not out of any religious conviction but because the Registry Office alternative seems somehow out of sync with the key experience. And regardless of the faith of the deceased, it would still be unthinkable for most non-practising Irish Catholics not to insist on the church rituals of death and burial.

What I'm saying is that there is, for a number of complicated reasons, an intersection between the way we live and the Catholic experience. There is a mix of experience and memory, of ritual and celebration, of life and worship that is still part of the lived experience of most Catholics, nominal or otherwise. It would be more than a pity, if our present experience of the Catholic Church was to force us to ditch the Catholic Experience which is still at the heart of so much of Irish life.

I know that just as there is a corpus of psychological wisdom that is immune to the excesses of popular psycho-babble, there is a corpus of great Art that stands on its own claiming its space in the great hall of learning. But apart from that, what are the standards or tools that help people to judge what has merit or what has not?

But is it art?

There's a story told – completely apocryphal, of course – about a group of amateur enthusiasts who decided to publish a new magazine. Words and phrases like 'intellectually credible', 'breaking new ground', 'significant', 'serious-minded' and so forth peppered the conversation. It was agreed that the first issue had to communicate the high seriousness with which the enterprise was undertaken. A painting by a well-known and highly respected artist was discussed and eventually accepted as appropriate for a first cover.

On the day of the launch, a discriminating guest mentioned to a member of the editorial committee that, in his view, the painting was upside down. A hastily-assembled meeting was called while the editorial committee turned the cover this way and that wondering, suggesting, reassuring but ultimately not knowing. Even though the same group had spent hours praising the painting, no one was quite sure whether, as a child might say, it was the right way up. Eventually it was discovered that it was neither up nor down but, through yet another misadventure with modern technology, inside out.

It was an instructive lesson. Does anyone really know about art? Does anyone, apart from a small group of enthusiasts, really care? Does art matter? What is art anyway?

I remember once being invited to a dinner-party in New York. It was full of 'art', bought, I suspect, by the square foot. The paint was in layers, caked as if it had been poured out of the tin, allowed to dry and then slashed with a sharp instrument. It was called *Intemperance*. In the corner of the apartment was a children's potty with a string attached to it running up to the ceiling. I was reluctant to enquire what it was called or what it might represent.

I know that just as there is a corpus of psychological wisdom that is immune to the excesses of popular psycho-babble, there is a corpus of great *Art* that stands on its own claiming its space in the great hall of learning. But apart from that, what are the standards or tools that help people to judge what has merit or what has not. I was recently brought through an art gallery where 'sculptures' were exhibited. Some were empty frames at the centre of which was a bit of textile and a piece of wood hammered into the wall with a caption underneath like *Bonniconlon Morning* (£2,500). What is all this about? What is it for? And can anyone make one for £2,500?

Clearly distinctions can be made between art and 'art'. Michelangelo's masterpiece in the Sistine Chapel is widely regarded as the greatest feat of painting in the history of the world but what of Andy Warhol's silk screen reproduction of a photograph of Marilyn Monroe? Or Chris Ofili's splattering the Virgin Mary with elephant dung? Was Michaelangelo in the business of art and Warhol in the art business? Is it any longer art when an artist surrenders to mechanism and accident by presenting an unmade bed as a central metaphor?

In a contribution to *The Observer*, Andrew Marr once suggested that the director of the National Gallery in London, Neil MacGregor had 'a problem of barbarism.' The problem is that an increasingly atheist, or agnostic, population hasn't the knowledge or vocabulary to appreciate the subtleties of a religious faith embedded in so much art.

So art is being viewed 'with the original point of it scooped out.' The point is that we can't approach great religious paintings as if they were just formal moments in the history of art. Unless we have the inner language and meaning to understand their content and context then we end up in a discussion about form and technique.

To illustrate, Bryan Appleyard in *The Sunday Times* points to Francisco de Zurbaran's painting *The Bound Lamb*. This shows a lamb with his feet tied. In any culture, it is a pitiful scene, the impending slaughter of an innocent lamb, but in a Christian culture, it is viewed as a metaphor for the sufferings of Christ, the Lamb of God. The painting may work in its own terms and at a surface level but without the perspective of understanding and knowledge it loses much of its impact.

In a sense this is really asking what art is. Art is about beauty, truth, meaning, communication but are there canons of excellence that help us define its value or is it merely about sensation or preference? Are there ground rules which should help us to decipher art from, for want of a better word, non-art?

The difficulty is that this vocabulary too is inaccessible to so many today. For many art is a way of engaging with life at a fundamental level. It is a medium, in Marr's phrase, 'encrusted with serious questions about life', with a moral and human seriousness but it is not naturally susceptible to immediate or widespread understanding. But how do we connect with art if we don't know what to look for, if we don't know what words to use? And how can we know unless someone shows us? But in this post-modernist age, where there is no agreed wisdom on anything, the question is still there - what is *Art*?

Priests of my vintage find ourselves caught between two generations: older priests who never felt quite at home with the vision of Vatican II and younger priests basking in the new conservatism sweeping the church. And those squeezed in between are a lost tribe, waving our tattered flags after the war. It is the dying of the light; the morning after optimism.

The lost dreamers

ONE of the best known priests in England, Oliver McTernan, has left the priesthood. Well, yes and no. Yes, in the sense that he no longer works as a priest in the active ministry. No, in the sense that he believes he is still living out his priesthood to the full. It's a transition, he says, rather than a departure.

His leaving is widely regarded as a great loss. A PP in Notting Hill in West London for over twenty years, McTernan built up a congregation that was ethnically and socially diverse and succeeded in getting a high level of lay participation in running the parish. At the same time he was involved in a number of national initiatives and was a regular contributor to BBC Radio Four's *Thought for the Day*.

While he insists that he is not disillusioned and that his faith is as strong as ever he says he is frightened to stay on in active ministry because, as he told *The Tablet*, he has seen so many of his friends 'turn almost into eccentrics because they kept trying to carry on in isolation.'

It's the isolation that, in the end, gets to people of McTernan's vintage. In his mid-Fifties, he is one of the Vatican II generation of priests who now find themselves progressively out of sync with the Church they were ordained into. Seminary training and ordination were part of the great wave of optimism that came with Vatican II.

There was to be a return to the roots - literally, a radicalism - and a letting go of the accretions of past centuries that had lost the run of themselves and falsely insinuated themselves into the centre. Collegiality, co-responsibility, a people's church - these were the buzz-words that tried to put flesh on a new but old theology.

But now the dream is over, killed with a thousand cuts. Not least the failure of the clerical church to introduce the structures that would give substance to what the theology meant; not least the circling of the wagons as leaders lost their nerve and their faith in what God's Spirit was saying to the church; and not least the restoration policies of recent years.

I know because I've been there, done that. I'm part of McTernan's generation, part of the lost dream and one of the lost dreamers. The priest-poet Pádraig J. Daly is another and his poem, *The Lost Dreamers,*• charts our progress:

> *We began in bright certainty*
> *Your will was a master plan*
> *Lying open before us.*
> *Sunlight blessed us,*
> *Fields of birds sang for us,*
> *Rainfall was your kindness tangible.*
> *But our dream was flawed;*
> *And we hold it now,*
> *Not in ecstacy but in dogged loyalty,*
> *Waving our tattered flags after the war*
> *Helping the wounded across the desert.*

Now priests of my vintage find ourselves caught between two generations: older priests who never felt quite at home with the vision of Vatican II and younger priests basking in the new conservatism sweeping the church. And those squeezed in between are a lost tribe, waving our tattered flags after the war. It is the dying of the light; the morning after optimism.

And what's happening now is not just that vocations are dwindling and that priests are ageing but that among the middle generation a great disillusionment has set in and many, like McTernan, are drifting away from the institutional church.

The Vatican II crop, if you like, is visibly thinning on the ground as it feels itself pressed, on the one side, by the clericalism and authoritarianism of the older generation of priests and, on the other side, by the growth of a new clericalism and authoritarianism among younger priests. And on top of that everything in the post-Vatican II church is now officially seen in black and white - there are no more areas of grey. Life is simple - and that's official.

My generation of priests feels very much on their own, caught between two generations and more and more are giving up the fight. Generally speaking there's no progressive spirit among the younger clergy. There's no openness, no exciting grasp of or adherence to the theology of Vatican II. Rather there's a hierarchical and authoritarian approach to church and parish which runs not just against the theology of Vatican II but the spirit of our age and this has the effect in not connecting with and, in effect, alienating many people.

In a sense McTernan is just accepting the logic of what has happened. He tells a story about the late Bishop Christopher Butler who, standing on the steps of St Peter's in Rome at the end of Vatican II, said that it would take thirty or forty years to implement the changes. A year or two before Butler died McTernan asked him for his current assessment - he had revised it to one hundred and forty years! The morning after optimism and the dying of the light?

No wonder priests like McTernan are drifting away from the church. Not to speak of all those who have left but haven't gone. ·

• The Lost Dreamers / Dedalus 1999

We remember long, hot summers with molten tar squeezing up between our toes, the slaking of thirsts at a mountain stream, the taste of tea on the bog, the free-wheeling towards home as the sun's rays lengthened on a July evening, the sights and the sounds of what, at least at this distance, appears an idyllic childhood. The last thing we could have imagined was that any adult could possibly represent any danger to us.

The end of innocence

IT isn't surprising that so many were surprised when last year Gardaí in Middleton issued a statement to the effect that a post-mortem had revealed that 11-year-old Robert Holohan had not been sexually assaulted. The presumption was that some sex-crazed paedophile had abducted Robert, sexually abused him and dumped his body. That presumption was fuelled by the tabloids reporting that a list of paedophiles had been prepared by Gardaí as possible suspects.

In the event, the truth was considerably less dramatic. A young man gave himself up was been charged with manslaughter. It appears that there was no intention to kill, that in whatever encounter took place something went badly wrong and the young man panicked. None of the nightmare scenarios laid out so graphically by the tabloids materialised. It's probably no comfort to Robert's parents but, in the long run, it may be something of a consolation that his final hours where not as the tabloids had expected or anticipated.

Regardless, it marks the end of innocence. We had come to a point where we presumed that the death of the two young girls at Soham in England was replicated here in Ireland. The half-hearted effort of some papers to create a fuss about a few British-registered vehicles sighted in the area affected a belief that the worst possible scenario was somehow more in keeping with people who weren't Irish.

While the nation held its breath, we knew that we had crossed another line in the sand. Our economic success, the sexualisation of society, easy access to pornography as well as increasing mobility, more disposable income and extra leisure have all contributed to the Americanisation of our society, where anything goes as long as you want it and can pay for it. We know now that anything can happen, that the lurid exaggerations of the tabloids could have come true. And possibly will, one day.

There was a time when we imagined that we could have given our children the childhoods we all had: cycling around the roads, exploring the countryside, playing the innocent games. There was a time when we imagined that we could facilitate that childhood innocence when wonder and trust and security were taken for granted. Now we know that day is gone.

Whether childhood was always as innocent as we sometimes imagine in retrospect is another question. Memory sieves out the negative. Retrospection accentuates the positive. Everyone couldn't possibly have been happy all the time but looking back we somehow imagine that they were.

We remember long, hot summers with molten tar squeezing up between our toes, the slaking of thirsts at a mountain stream, the taste of tea on the bog, the free-wheeling towards home as the sun's rays lengthened on a July evening, the sights and the sounds of what, at least at this distance, appears an idyllic childhood. The last thing we could have imagined was that any adult could possibly represent any danger to us. The biggest worry we had was that some adult would report some misdemeanour to our parents. That seemed the only good reason to give adults a wide berth.

But now no one can afford that type of childhood. Now parents have to warn their children about the dangers of any kind of contact with unknown or even well known adults. Now everyone dealing with children has to ensure that, in so far as is humanly possible, everyone everywhere all the time has to be supervised. Common sense suggests it. Society is intent on ensuring it. And, more to the point, the safety of children demands it.

We may mourn the loss of such innocence. We may regret that children won't be as carefree and instinctive as they might. But the truth is that we can't turn back the clock. Children are maturing earlier. They see more than their young minds can reasonably be expected to deal with. They know more than we knew at twice their age. They are at ease with technology. They question everything. They see different worlds opening up to them on television. They are old before their time.

We may lament that reality but we can't change it. We can, in a given set of circumstances, control children's access to bits of that world. But there is no other world now for them to grow up in. No idyllic countryside where we can safely let them wander and explore. No place where they can be safe.

The world is a village now, for better or worse. And children want their place in it. Parents may be able for a time to moderate or deflect or distract but children come back to the question unerringly. They will always want to know why.

The grim reality for parents today is that children have to be told difficult truths that they will struggle to get their minds around. In an ideal world we can fantasise about replicating the idyllic childhoods of the past, but the horrible truth is that we can no longer afford that fantasy. Life is cruel and unfortunately children have to be told that too. Not telling them is to imagine we live in a different world. The end of innocence indeed.

Thirty years on, a full tide has gone out for the Roman Catholic Church in Ireland. The most obvious truth is that we have failed, indeed refused to manage change. The road-map that God gave us to find our way in a changing world has been torn up into little pieces by clerical gods who refused to accept its import.

Taking the tide

I was ordained a priest over thirty years ago. Just after the Second Vatican Council the message ringing in my ears was that the Roman Catholic Church was anxious to connect with modern culture, engage with the world, renew its structures. The buzz words were 'co-responsibility', 'collaboration', 'collegiality' and the expectation was that they would transmute into their modern cousins, 'Openness', 'Transparency' and 'Accountability.' A new church for a new world.

At the time ninety per cent of Catholics attended weekly Mass; seminaries were full; bishops, priests and religious had the wind on their backs. Why change a winning formula? Well, this time our church had read the signs of the times. Or so we thought.

Thirty years on, a full tide has gone out for the Roman Catholic Church in Ireland. Attendance at Mass is in free-fall; vocations have virtually disappeared; and, after a recurring nightmare of betrayals of public and private trusts, our credibility is at floor level. Now the wind is on our faces and the hill is rising before us.

There are many reasons for this: incompetent leadership, maladministration, over-reliance on centralised control and legal solutions, a secretive church culture. But the most obvious truth is that we have failed, indeed refused to manage change. We underestimated the need for radical change; we refused to trust those who could have driven change; and the road-map that God gave us to find our way in a changing world has been torn up into little pieces by clerical gods who refused to accept its import. Now as the institutional church implodes around us we recognise the price we have paid for the philosophy and actions of those who have insisted on turning us again in the dismal direction of the Council of Trent.

If you sense a mounting anger in my words, you read them well. Because, after more than thirty years of priesting, it is clear that the Roman Catholic Church in Ireland is dying on its feet. It gives me no pleasure to say that. And I know that many others, from within the Church, will read my words as a form of disloyalty and betrayal. But I make no apology for them. Nor should I.

If, in the wake of the Council, we had owned the road-map, we would have put in place a structure that would have turned our church into a people-driven institution with a participative and collaborative ethos, a structure that would have built into it processes for dealing with the failures of the past, an analysis of present needs and a way of devising strategies for the future.

That didn't happen because there was a failure in leadership among bishops and clergy, a lack of commitment to and a palpable discomfort with the road-map of the Second Vatican Council and a disheartening return to an ethos of control and infallibility.

In short, the change that would have allowed the Catholic Church to engage imaginatively with a changing world was torpedoed by bishops and clergy. We refused to let go. And now we are reaping the whirlwind of that failure.

My conviction is that, even now, we need to ask the hard questions and to name the hard truths. Why is the Irish Catholic Church so out of touch with the lived experience of its people? Why did the clerical church see the developing role of the laity as a threat to its power? How did so many highly intelligent, moral and committed church-people get it so wrong over child abuse? What prevents us from recognising the changing face of authority and the changing demands of church leadership? Why are we afraid to explore the darkness at the heart of priesthood? Why was the energy and vision of the Second Vatican Council strangled at birth? Why have we so much difficulty with concepts like accountability and democracy? Why has an aged, male, celibate, clerical coterie to control everything, to decide everything?

We need to embrace change so that we can remake, re-create, re-imagine a new and very different Church: a Church that listens to itself by listening to its people; a Church that loosens the stranglehold of control exercised by the clergy and releases the gifts of lay people; a Church that facilitates new forms of authority and leadership; a Church that makes celibacy in priesthood a voluntary choice; a Church that opens up a debate on women priests; a Church in tune with the rhythms of our time; a Church that cherishes diversity and celebrates difference; a Church that names the truth, regardless; a Church that implements the teachings of the Second Vatican Council rather than ambushes them along the way.

A feudal church is incapable of conversing with today's world and unless we change radically the Irish Roman Catholic Church will just continue to die.

The truth is that much of what is written is trite, ephemeral, a waste of time. Just as much, if not most of what appears on television is trite, ephemeral, a waste of time. For every Big Brother there is a Sean Ó Mordha, for every The Bingo Show there's Questions and Answers. The cliché is actually true – television is just a window on the world.

No such thing as a mass audience

CLIVE James started it all. Making fun of television. Once people waited for television critics to confirm or deny their prognosis. Like the urbane Raymond Williams, complaining about the seamless web of unmeaning he perceived 'the flow of television' had become. But after Clive's celebrated tenure as *The Observer's* television critic, a once respected genre became little more than an opportunity to mock its main participants.

The result is that television criticism is now seen as a form of entertainment. At its best, it can be clever and witty, as with A.A. Gill in *The Sunday Times;* at its worst, it can be tedious and abusive as with Liam Fay in the same paper. The sense is that all this drivel is really beneath us but it's there and someone has to explain how insignificant it is.

Unlike books. Books are significant and book reviews are important. Even though, in the incestuous literary scene in Ireland, A reviews B's book this week, C reviews A's book next week and B reviews C's book the week after, there's a curious assumption that this patent form of literary aggrandisment is mean to be taken seriously.

To be a paid-up member of the middle-class literati, you read books but you don't watch television. That's the legend. Even if you have to pretend that you've read the books and not watched the television. The reality is usually more perverse. Few people actually read the books they buy and many even pretend they've read the books they don't buy. Most people watch television but appear intent on convincing themselves that they don't, really, because there's nothing on it worth watching. Even though they could successfully compete in *Mastermind* - chosen subject, the plot-lines of Coronation Street 1963 - 1999. A bit like the late Malcom Muggeridge appearing on television in order to explain the futility of television to the great unwashed.

Attend any of those depressing summer schools or a grand conference with a suitably pretentious title and ten-to-one you'll bump into a series of predictable statements about the culturally deleterious effect of television. Or the fact that so much of it is so ephemeral and mind-numbing. Or that standards have slipped in the perceived dumbing down of the media in general. Some may even grandly inform anyone who cares to listen that they've thrown out their television set, usually in a lake somewhere. In some quarters it's the in-thing to do.

But no one would say the same about books - burning them or throwing them in a lake. It's *de rigeur* that the written word is significant, that there's almost a sacred space it occupies in a civilised life. Yet no one would claim that every written word makes sense, that every book is a significant contribution to the sum of knowledge, that *The Irish Mirror* is the same as *The Irish Times,* that *How to spend your SSIA* money is the same league as John McGahern's *'Memoir'.*

The truth is that much of what is written is trite, ephemeral, a waste of time. Just as much, if not most of what appears on television is trite, ephemeral, a waste of time. For every *Big Brother* there is a Sean O Mordha, for every *The Bingo Show* there's *Questions and Answers.* The cliché is actually true - television is just a window on the world. That's it. It's a universal language, not an art-form. Television just is. All you need to do is sit in front of it. And those who open the window, like opening a book, will do with it what they please. And like reading a book, most people will measure the truth television presents against their own experience.

If people are taken in by advertisments suggesting that by placing electronic pads on their tummys at regular intervals most of their stomachs will miraculously disappear, they are going to be taken in anyway by a door-to-door salesman offering some other magical potion. It's not television's fault that the values of a consumer society are in the ascendant or that less people read or that religion is in decline. People make choices and if they want to read *The News of the World* and watch *Fair City*, then they are entitled to their trivia in a free society.

The problem with television is that it is easily parodied and effortlessly patronised. The logic of a certain kind of intellectual snobbery is that the generality of people cannot be trusted to make up their own minds but that highly intelligent people can make the important and appropriate distinctions. Intelligence is of course comparative but if the legal system for dispensing justice through the jury system rests on the wisdom of the average person, then surely the same logic applies to television. And that truth comes out in the wash.

Of course programmes can be slanted and choices can be influenced as in any other communications media. But when the camera moves in people tend to make up their own minds. In the Northern Troubles of the last few decades, both sides were able to feed their own propaganda machines when the cameras were around. But the pictures coming from Belfast had the effect too of turning armchair, closet republicans in the south into supporters of the peace process. Charlie McCreevy once appeared on *The Late Late Show* in a damage limitation exercise after his last budget but all the huffing-and-puffing didn't disguise the arrogance that consistently undoes him on television.

Rabble-rousing doesn't work on television. It translates as rant. Tyrants, Camus said, conduct monologues above a million solitudes. The magic of television is that it makes it impossible, for anyone, to be above people because on television, despite the packages, the essential comes through. Television carries its own very accessible truth.

What's important about television is not, as I said earlier, that criticism has become a form of entertaining blather, but that the nature of television is that everyone is their own critic. Those who have theories about the debilitating effects of television on the alienated masses will have to review their convenient hypotheses. There is no such thing as a mass television audience. Just individuals, often millions of them, pressing their remote controls.

Now let's see what's Homer's problem this week. Homer? You know, Mr. Simpson.

Others didn't know why they stopped. They intended to go and they would be very upset if someone said they no longer practiced their religion but somehow they just didn't seem to get there that often anymore. Going to church had become a bit like intending to take more exercise or going on a diet or being good. Like in other areas of life there can be a significant gap between intention and performance.

Not going to Church anymore

A free copy of a novel by Maeve Binchy came with an Irish Sunday paper. Indeed part of the marketing of Sunday papers now is to include some give-away: CDs, DVDs, special holiday offers and the like. If you want to attract new readers or even hold old ones, the wisdom seems to be, you have to give them a little bit extra. It seems that a little bribe, if that's not too strong a word for it, can influence our decisions or even change our habits.

No wonder that some imaginative church-people are going down the same road. In Manchester a few weeks ago, Church of England churches gave out bars of chocolate as part of a 'Back to Church' initiative. Worshippers were encouraged to invite someone who didn't regularly go to church to pick up a bar of chocolate and to stay on for Sunday Worship.

As all the mainline Christian churches are leaking worshippers it seems that we need to employ some imaginative response if we are going to stem the drift. Hence the bars of chocolate. And even if it all seems a bit unusual, even pathetic in a way, at least there's some lateral thinking going on. And some attention being given to a growing problem.

A few years ago some important research was carried out into why people no longer go to church. It emerged in a book called *Gone but Not Forgotten* by Philip Richter and Leslie Francis. Richter and Francis surveyed those who no longer went to church and asked them why they stopped going.

A number of reasons emerged: some had begun to doubt; some had lost whatever bit of faith they had; some had been offended by something the preacher said; and so on. Most however had fallen out of the habit, playing golf on a Sunday morning or bringing their children to swimming or visiting Granny and somewhere in the mix going to church slid down the list of priorities.

Others didn't know why they stopped. They intended to go and they would be very upset if someone said they no longer practiced their religion but somehow they just didn't seem to get there that often anymore. Going to church had become a bit like intending to take more exercise or going on a diet or being good. Like in other areas of life there can be a significant gap between intention and performance.

It's inevitable that some people will lose their faith or decisively abandon the religious enterprise but my sense is that a huge percentage of those who no longer go to church are among the 'Don't knows'. And that offers a considerable challenge to the Christian churches.

In the old days, in the Catholic tradition, if people stopped going to Mass, the local priest or a neighbour might have a word with them. Or, more decisively and sometimes alarmingly, when a parish mission came around the local PP would set an enthusiastic Redemptorist on the few recalcitrants. Nowadays, either response would be regarded as unduly intrusive, even an inappropriate invasion of people's private space, if nor bizarre.

But the difficulty now is that if there is no response to those who slide away from community worship that lack of response can be interpreted as disinterest on the part of the church. Do we not care?

If a significant percentage of people are losing contact with their religion, how can the Church respond caringly and sensitively to those who need to be told that their presence in church is missed? Perhaps we need some version of the Manchester bar of chocolate to draw attention to the gradual slide away from church. That might create a bit of space to allow friends, in a caring and non-combative way, to encourage those who have moved from practice to non-practice and probably haven't noticed that much.

A feature of the modern slide is that, even in church-going families, children with the implicit support of their parents have decided themselves not to go. Weekend Masses now in many parishes have very few children attending and when it comes to First Communion many of them have not been to church since their baptism. That's true of course of children of parents who never come to church but progressively it's also true of children of parents who go to Mass every Sunday. Sometimes I look down at a congregation on a Saturday night or a Sunday morning and I wonder: where are all the children? Why are they not here? What's keeping them away? If it is unthinkable not to send them to school, how has it become acceptable not to bring them to Mass, even when their parents go?

Clearly, as well as encouraging people to think again about going to Mass on Sundays, we need to do some creative and imaginative thinking about making our churches more welcoming and our liturgies more receptive to people's needs - including children's needs. Initial areas that need our attention are participation, sermons and music and worship that directly connect with people's experiences.

What a pity that so many are slipping away from communal worship of a God in whom so many still profess to believe? The loss is theirs and ours too.

Little wonder that there are waiting lists of more than a year for the €160,000 Porsche 911. Or that well-to-do women are queueing up to buy €5,000 handbags in Brown Thomas in Dublin. Or that the new lifestyle is about spend, spend, spend. And wanting everything now. There's no such thing anymore as delayed pleasure.

The spend generation

SHOPPING, someone said, is the new religion. As the Catholic Church cuts down on numbers of Masses due to the ageing and declining numbers of priests and the old religion contracts, the new religion is expanding by the day with supermarkets staying open around the clock. With full employment, low interest rates and the presumption that the good times are here to stay, people are spending, spending, spending.

Frugality is now a bad word. *Making-ends-meet* is a historical term from somewhere this side of the Famine. Temperance in lifestyle has been defeated by increasing levels of disposable income. And we only save, as with the SSIAs, if the government gives us a bonanza of 25% interest over five years.

Little wonder that there are waiting lists of more than a year for the €160,000 Porsche 911. Or that well-to-do women are queueing up to buy €5,000 handbags in Brown Thomas in Dublin. Or that the new lifestyle is about spend, spend, spend. And wanting everything now. There's no such thing anymore as delayed pleasure.

Take my friend Jimmy (not his real name). Jimmy is 25, a plasterer making over €600 on a bad week, a good week can get him €1,000. He tells me, and I have no reason to doubt him, that at the end of the week all the money is gone. He blames the cost of living, or more particularly the price of drink. I blame Jimmy.

This is how he explains the present critical state of his finances. He just has 'to go out' four nights event week. First there's the taxi to the pub. Then there's an inordinate number of pints of Guinness followed by 'shorts', presumably when his distended blather begins to object to the excess and after a night, completed by the requisite Take-Away meal from a chipper and the taxi home Jimmy has no change out of €100. Some nights he ends up in a disco with his girlfriend and that means a taxi home for her and for him as well as an extra Take-Away. At the beginning of some weeks, he tells me, he's so short of cash that he has to tap his mother for a few euros. But he always pays her back. He always pays her back, he repeats. He's not a skin-flint - the ultimate anti-social slur, apparently.

Jimmy could own his own house by this, drive a better car and do considerably less damage to his health if there was an inch of self-control in his system. But, as he tells me, the crack is mighty and that seems to be all that matters. He's on a merry-go-round of excess, splashing out his cash as if there's no tomorrow. And spending not just his own cash but the money he borrowed from the bank on foreign holidays (at least two every year and, again, 'mighty crack' apparently) and there's always the credit card that sees him paying enormous levels of interest. But sure, you know yourself.

The truth is, dear reader, as you and I know, wise owls and solid citizens that we are, there is a tomorrow and with Jimmy, you and I will be paying for it. Give him a few more years when the ready money from the plastering disappears or his arms are no longer able to stand the strain and the bank is keeping him at arms length and all the credit is used up on the credit-card and his present girlfriend is the mother of his children, where will Jimmy be? Yes, I know. Jimmy will be top of some queue for social housing.

With a bit of foresight, a modicum of control and a re-negotiation of his finances, Jimmy could turn his present earning power into permanent assets, like a house. But like the rest of the Irish nation he's on a merry-go-round of spend, spend, spend. If the pub isn't open there's always the off-license; if the shop is closed, you can buy on the internet; if the cash flow is slow, then get it from the bank.

Expectations have grown enormously in recent years. In the dim and distant past, like the 1960s, couples rarely owned their own houses when they married and if they did, all they could afford to furnish was the kitchen and the bedroom and completing the house took the best part of a lifetime. Now the house has to be finished and furnished to the highest standards before couples would consider moving in to it. A few years ago few couples could afford to go out any night of the week and second cars and second holidays - even first holidays - were unknown luxuries. Once we cut our cloth to fit our measure now we're ordering all kinds of exotica, beyond our means and, if the truth be told, beyond our needs.

There's no such thing as saving anymore for the rainy day. The wisdom is that money is losing value so spend it as soon as you can and there'll be no more rainy days because, as part of the euro club, interest rates will remain low. And what hope have the Jimmys of this world when big business, the banks, the media, advertising and envy conspire to part him from his money.

But somewhere in the distance, as we slip the BMW out of the paved driveway of a house beyond our means, there's a small, still voice asking the same insistent questions: Is this all there is? My parents had none of this. And am I any happier than my parents were?

What seems extraordinary to me is the assumption that believing in nothing makes more sense than believing in something. Or believing that some things are right and some things are wrong is less intelligent than seeing everything as a matter of personal choice or individual whim. Or that believing in a God who loves us and cares us is something that narrows the horizon but believing in nothing opens us up to a new and wider world.

Believing in something

Have you noticed the way people nowadays often tend to distance themselves from religion, or from appearing religious, almost as if it was a virus at odds with reason and common sense? Terry Wogan, England's favourite Irishman, was at it recently. 'My parents' he told *The Sunday Times* 'were always too cynical about religion for me to go for the whole worship thing.' Lucky Terry. Spared all that Catholic guilt.

How often we hear that view repeated in interviews with the great and good. Phrases like 'I was born a Catholic but . . .' or 'I'm not religious myself . . .' are short-hand for establishing some kind of media credibility as an intelligent and reasonable member of the human race. Someone who has left behind the dead weight of religious belief for the bright open spaces of modern living.

It's almost as if, to be a citizen of the new world, we have to leave behind all that medieval rubbish we used to call religion. We've seen through it. We've outgrown it. Religion is off the modern agenda, a lost cause. It is as if you move yourself away from the centre of the modern stage by admitting to anything as dumb as religious belief. 'For God's sake', you hear someone say, with unconscious ambivalence, 'who believes in religion anymore?' Or someone who, having established his atheistic convictions, asks a priest to say a Mass for his late mother!

Many years ago the late John F. X. Harriott wrote that the idea that you have to be dumb to be religious was becoming the new intellectual slavery. And we seem to have reached that point. Religion, in sophisticated circles in Ireland today, is regarded as a lost cause and religious enthusiasts are often perceived as at best eccentrics, at worst dangerously disillusioned refugees from the nineteenth century.

You can see how this has happened. Once critics of religion pointed to the Crusades as indicative of the damage religion can do if you take it seriously. Now they point to the last decade in Ireland and the legacy of the clerical child sexual abuse scandals. Indeed many in Ireland have given themselves permission to jettison the practice of religion and to abandon a religious sense on the basis of the failures of individuals or institutions.

But inadequate or even scandalous Christians shouldn't discredit religion anymore than inadequate teachers discredit education or irresponsible journalists discredit the media. If you lose confidence in the butcher it seems an unnecessarily dramatic response to give up meat for life.

That's not to say that some people have arrived at a position of non-belief after giving the whole matter due consideration. And that's fair enough. But to dismiss the whole religious agenda as nonsensical because the prevailing current is now moving against it is in itself nonsensical.

Just because in some sophisticated circles religious belief is regarded as unsustainable or even embarrassing doesn't mean that for many people just down the road from that refined enclave a religious sense may give meaning and substance to their lives. Or that in other parts of the world religious belief is at the coalface of the fight for justice and dignity for the oppressed. Bigotry after all is not confined to religion.

I can understand how people arrive at a position of non-belief. I can see why the failures of individual Christians, for example, can turn others off religion. And I know that much of the clutter of modern life can crowd out a religious, even a spiritual sense.

But what seems extraordinary to me is the assumption that believing in nothing makes more sense than believing in something. Or that to stand beside a grave and believe in a new and different existence has less going for it than believing that we are no more than a pinch of dust. Or saying that we are unique individuals created and loved by a personal God is somehow less than accepting we're just incidental existences flitting momentarily across the sky. Or believing that some things are right and some things are wrong is less intelligent than seeing everything as a matter of personal choice or individual whim. Or that believing in a God who loves us and cares us is something that narrows the horizon but believing in nothing opens us up to a new and wider world.

Much of what presents as rejection of religion in Ireland today is often no more than a convenient alliance of the disillusioned, the sophisticated, the intellectually dishonest and the lazy. Seeing the bigger picture is not about rejecting religion (out of anger or a failure to swim against the tide) but recognising the richness a religious perspective brings to life. Surely what we're doing is throwing the baby out with the bathwater if the failures of individuals lead to the rejection of a religious sense?

It's one thing to arrive at an intellectual conviction that God doesn't exist or that religion makes no sense. It's quite another to dismiss religion as irrelevant and a religious sense as unimportant just because that's the current wheeze. Atheism is a form of religion too and it has its own bigots but let's not pretend that it has more going for it than God.

*Anonymous campaigns are born, not out of doing good but out of a
sulphurous mixture of envy, resentment and moral cowardice. They
sit somewhere, with malice aforethought, and coldly and calculatedly
take someone's character apart. And they address the envelope and
go to the Post Office and buy a stamp and send through the post
their contribution to the pain and hurt they insist on visiting on some
unsuspecting individual.*

A cowardly idiosyncracy

I made a rule for myself many years ago not to read anonymous letters.
I used to once - until I realised that by reading them I was conceding
a kind of victory to the writers of such letters. I was allowing them to
colonise a part of my life. Now I look for the name and if it's not there,
I look for the waste-paper basket.

It takes a bit of discipline not to read them. Curiosity is one thing.
Wanting to justify oneself is another. Then you spend the day
wondering who might possibly have written the anonymous bile and
you realise that you're doing exactly what they wanted you to do. An
important bit of freedom to claim, I've discovered, is not to allow the
dreary world of the anonymous letter writer to impinge on your day. Or
your life.

Anonymous letter-writers usually imagine that they occupy some
kind of moral high ground and have come to believe that their cowardly
idiosyncrasy is somehow in the service of party or ideology or even
God. But once you sample their bizarre contributions, you quickly
realise just how far they can go to lose whatever notion of respect and
decency they fondly imagine themselves to have. Usually they are
bitter and broken people, out of sync with themselves and the world,
unhappy and often twisted individuals carrying on a campaign to save

the world for whatever version of the truth they espouse.

The truth is that their anonymous campaigns are born, not out of doing good but out of a sulphurous mixture of envy, resentment and moral cowardice. They sit somewhere, with malice aforethought, and coldly and calculatedly take someone's character apart. And they address the envelope and go to the Post Office and buy a stamp and send through the post their contribution to the pain and hurt they insist on visiting on some unsuspecting individual. And then they sit back and wait for the suffering to happen.

Anonymous letter-writing is a form of moral cowardice. Anonymous phone calls too, though nowadays the technology is there to circumvent them. In the early days of the Caller Display Unit, when I was doing a late night radio programme for Mid West Radio I used to get phone calls upbraiding me for some comment I had made earlier. Sometimes the calls would come at 3 o'clock in the morning and, in my bleary-eyed state, the only satisfaction I could glean was to stop the ranter in full spate and say that I would call him or her back in the morning and wasn't their number 094 721?? At the time a small but important triumph that was, I remember, extremely satisfying!

Moral courage is often in short supply. And when it is, its sisters Respect and Decency get lost somewhere along the line - even when the comment is not anonymous. You know the sly, crafty and secretive individual who'd mind mice at a crossroads and is a dab hand at the half-remark, the deft insinuation, the sly comment that can shape a juicy bit of gossip out of the most unpromising of material. Knowing just how much to say and knowing where to say it is more than half the battle. Then the remark is taken up, carried a few miles, a theory is propounded and someone loses a reputation. Different technique, same result.

It's a strange thing. There were never more personality development courses. Never more psychological profiles to help us to understand what makes us tick. Never more navel-gazing to try to fathom who we are and where we're coming from.

We have journeys inwards, rooting around in our innards; journeys into the mind, digging deep into the psyche; journeys around and about ourselves, visiting the outer reaches of our sub-consciousness. And we never had more individuals dealing with stuff, naming it, claiming it, taming it, staying with it, confronting it, befriending it, owning it, sitting on it, seeing how it rests with them and a whole industry of psycho-babble helping us deal with our real and imaginary neuroses.

But is all this guff deflecting us from dealing with more basic realities that impinge more on the everyday lives we lead? Like, for example, concepts of respect and decency.

We recognise respect when we meet it. We have a built-in system for detecting what is or is not decent. We don't need a degree in psychology to work our way around these everyday concepts because respect and decency deal in the fundamentals of life. And, as the gurus would say, they rest easy with us.

One of the wonders of these forms of character assassination is the ability to hold together two completely opposing positions. Like the daily communicant who spends most of her waking hours looking for and spreading gossip about everyone and the juicier the gossip the more she enjoys disseminating it. Or the self-righteous individual who regularly lectures everyone on the absence of a sense of sin but who spends his time ferreting out even juicier scandals and taking away reputations, all the while tut-tutting away about the state of the church and the world.

Once you meet that kind of stuff you begin to search around for ordinary, honest-to God qualities like respect and decency and to cherish them unambiguously. Qualities too, like the moral courage to say your piece without fear or favour and to say it publicly. Naming it and owning it.

It doesn't take any remarkable degree of perspicuity to conclude that in future years Catholics will be divided into a minority who will attend Mass, pay their collections and support their parish and a greater majority who will continue to regard themselves as Catholics and who will expect the Catholic Church to provide minimal services for them – baptisms, marriages and funerals – the 'hatch, match and dispatch' syndrome.

Paying our way

It's no secret that support for the Catholic Church in Ireland has declined in recent years. Thirty years ago, for example, surveys indicated that 92% of Catholics attended Mass regularly. It was, I think, an impossibly optimistic figure especially when you factored in those who couldn't possibly be in church – the very young, the very old, the sick. The comparable figure now is 60%, still a bit optimistic, I think, with much lower figures in some parishes.

My own opinion is that Catholics nowadays fall into four groups: (i) those who attend Mass every weekend; (ii) those who attend regularly (every second or third or even fourth Sunday); (iii) those who attend irregularly (every 2 to 3 months or so); and (iv) those who never attend (except maybe on Christmas night). I estimate that about 40% are in the first category and 20% in the second.

In most parishes a core group of about 40% attend Mass. The indications are that the 40% figure will probably decrease in future years and of the 20% who now attend irregularly they will either attend more irregularly or cease to practice altogether.

It doesn't take any remarkable degree of perspicuity to conclude that in future years Catholics will be divided into a minority who will attend Mass, pay their collections and support their parish and a greater majority who will continue to regard themselves as Catholics and who will expect the Catholic Church to provide minimal services for them - baptisms, marriages and funerals - the 'hatch, match and dispatch' syndrome.

This poses a particular problem in terms of keeping in existence the basics of parish life - Mass, the sacraments, a church, a priest, etc. Who will pick up the tab for the hatch, match and dispatch Catholics?

At present I would estimate that about 30% of Catholics are, in effect, paying for the running of Catholic parishes. Not that attendance, as outlined in the second paragraph, reflects contribution. Sometimes it's possible to be both pious and stingy, as well as less pious and more generous! That means that 70% of Catholics contribute little or nothing to the running of their parishes and yet expect that if they have a funeral, there will be a priest to say the Mass (even though he won't get a stipend for his work), a church which will be clean, warm, insured and well maintained (even though they don't even ask who's picking up the tab for all that) and even a choir to sing.

At present the numbers and the money are still adequate to fund basic parish services. But we are coming to a point when the generosity of the few won't cover the needs of the many. As the minority paying the piper decreases and the majority calling the tune increases we are going to reach a point when the system will eventually collapse. It's not too far away. Soon the money will simply not be there to sustain the whole process.

So what can be done? In Germany citizens who register as Catholics pay on average about €900 a year through their taxes and that money is passed on to the Catholic Church. If Catholics don't want to pay to their Church they are de-registered. This means that the services of the Catholic church are not available to them. For example they can't get married in a Catholic Church unless they are registered Catholics.

I'm not suggesting that the Minister for Finance should take up our collections for us. Or that we should stop burying people who don't pay their collections. But there's something to be said for adopting some system of registration for Catholics in Ireland so that the growing number of non-practising (and non-contributing) Catholics are not piggy-backing on the generosity of a declining number of practising (and contributing) Catholics. Sooner or later some distinction will have to be made between those who are paid up members of parishes and those who are not.

How to do that is the problem. Should there be, for those who are non-registered, non-practising, non-contributing, a list of charges say for a church wedding: (i) for doing the paperwork, say €100; (ii) for the use of the church, say €100; (iii) for heating, lighting and cleaning the Church, say €100; (iv) for the rehearsal, say €100; (v) for the priest conducting the ceremony, say €150; (vi) for the priest's attendance at the reception, say €100. And, of course, for those who are registered, contributing and practising Catholics, such charges would be waived.

I can hear some voices clambering in protest. €650! Some saying its too much. Some saying it's not half enough. After all it's only half what the flowers often cost. And less than the drinks for the toast. And less than the photographer. Others will say that it will only further alienate those who have already drifted away from the Church.

But how long will those who are now paying continue to pay for other people's weddings and funerals and baptisms? How long will we place our resources at the disposal of those whose interest in the Catholic Church doesn't extend much further than getting their church weddings on the cheap.

It's time for them to pay their way.

The Catholic Church had an inordinate influence in civil affairs in Ireland. Sometimes that suited the Catholic Church and sometimes that suited the State. And sometimes it wasn't possible to know where one started and the other ended. But there's a growing sense among church-people that the alliance in Ireland, since the foundation of the State, between Maynooth and Leinster House, hasn't served the Catholic Church well.

Privilege is bad for us

AT a meeting of more than a thousand members of the Vintners Association, Dan O'Keeffe, a publican from Dingle berated the government's anti-smoking policy. 'Who runs this country?' he asked. A long pause followed, while the immensity of the question sank in. Then he answered his own question: 'We do!' From the cheer that followed it was clear that the assembled publicans agreed.

We pride ourselves in Ireland on the accessibility of our politicians. It's part of our tradition - a result too of how small and self-contained the State is. Everyone knows someone who knows someone. Politicians hold clinics in pubs, press the flesh, have to be seen to be personable. One of our own.

But part of the problem we have is that this very closeness of the State to the people gives us an unwarranted belief in the influence we can exert. Dan O'Keeffe may well be right - the publicans may actually run the country - and indeed that perception is widely held. Or the GAA. Or the Catholic Church.

The Catholic Church, most would say now, had an inordinate influence in civil affairs in Ireland. Sometimes that suited the Catholic Church and sometimes that suited the State. And sometimes it wasn't possible to know where one started and the other ended. But there's a growing sense among church-people that the alliance in Ireland, since the foundation of the State, between Maynooth and Leinster House, hasn't served the Catholic Church well.

In Ireland, because the vast majority of citizens have been Catholics and because the Catholic Church had legions of volunteers, religious and lay, whom the State was happy to use for its own purposes, effectively the Catholic Church became an adjunct of the State - or some might say the other way round!

The Catholic Church was effectively the 'established Church' and it made a kind of sense that a provision in de Valera's Constitution, since abolished in a referendum, gave the Catholic Church a 'special status.' Even though Catholic bishops weren't invited to take seats in the Senate (like Church of Ireland bishops in the House of Lords), we were in everything but name the established Church. Now we wonder whether we had too much power for our own good.

In Britain at the moment, there's some soul-searching into the role of the Church of England (COE) as the 'established' Church. Part of the reason is that not everyone in the COE is looking forward to Prince Charles becoming King and automatically 'Supreme Governor of the Church of England and Defender of the Faith.' It's not just that many feel the prince's marital status, quite apart from the recent publicity, falls short of setting an appropriate example to the nation but that he seems to have little enough interest in religion. He would, he said once, prefer to see himself as 'Defender of Faith' than as 'Defender of the Faith'.

But the soul-searching into the wisdom of the COE being the 'established Church' goes much deeper than that. Now COE people are wondering about what price is being paid for the perception of entrenched privilege involved in their nominated membership of the Lords. Privilege, retired COE Bishop Mark Santer, wrote recently is 'bad for us.'

There could be a message there for the Catholic Church in Ireland. Have we deferred too much to our politicians? Have the boundaries between politics and religion been blurred with little service to God or State? In paying attention to the concerns of the State and the perks that followed have we contrived to dull the cutting edge of the Word of

God? Have we lost more than we gained by our astuteness as children of the world rather than of the Light?

I've always found it uncomfortable when civil and political dignitaries are given undue attention at what are, after all, religious services. Some years ago, on the occasion of a bishop's ordination, a Mayo politician, a Minister at the time, not known for his modesty, walked up the Cathedral with the swagger of a man who believed (and expected everyone else to believe) that the whole proceedings would have ground to a halt if he hadn't arrived.

Some would say that it's only good manners or good citizenship or good public relations to curry favour with the State and its public officials. And that's true. But, in so doing, sometimes the Church can compromise itself, can lose its independence and credibility, can divest itself of its real power, the power of the gospel message of Jesus Christ.

Because it is the nature of the Church and the gospel that to be true to what we believe we have to live at an angle to the world. We have to be an awkward presence forever questioning the status quo, the accepted wisdom. The history of religion tells us time and time again that once the Church becomes an accepted part of the social and political set-up, we've lost our way.

Mark Santer is right. Privilege is bad for us.

In Ireland, humour isn't accorded due respect or status.
While we acknowledge easily enough the value of humour as a
distraction, a safety valve, a necessary antidote to a contrived
seriousness, we don't afford it any great significance.

Our God giggles

AMONG the national characteristics we don't share with our nearest neighbour is a respect for a sense of humour. Indeed there's a case to be made that, for the English, humour is part of the very vocabulary of Englishness, part of the language they use to communicate the values they hold dear. It would be difficult to imagine writers like Shakespeare, Chaucer, Jane Austen, Dickens, even Thackeray, without the leaven of humour. And with the War, the incorrigible cheerfulness of the English, as Hitler's bombs rained down on them, was part of a concerted effort not to concede anything to Germany, even a psychological advantage, as the plucky inhabitants of London and Liverpool got on with their lives. Indeed, in later years, the BBC television series, *Dad's Army*, summed up the lively sense of the ridiculous and the underlying respect for humour that became something of a national characteristic. Laughing at themselves became a way of life, a necessary camouflage for the terrible context in which they lived.

In Ireland, humour isn't accorded the same respect or status. While we acknowledge easily enough the value of humour as a distraction, a safety valve, a necessary antidote to a contrived seriousness, we don't afford it any great significance. It would be difficult, for example, to imagine the FCA or even the Irish army being given the *Dad's Army* treatment. And the continued failure of RTE television to produce anything remotely like a successful comedy series confirms the point. The kind of under-stated, faintly ridiculous, but beautifully observed mockery that made *Yes, Prime Minister* such a success is quite simply beyond us. While we are surrounded with comic possibilities and we never needed the leaven of humour more, there is no audience for a *Dublin Opinion*. That gentle, mocking, disrespectful grace is not part of the national lexicon.

Part of the difficulty is that we are a small, and for that reason, vulnerable, entity with an almost insatiable need to be liked, even loved. We haven't the confidence that size brings. So we want to believe the carefully constructed myths about supposed national characteristics like hospitality, generosity and so on that Bord Fáilte, among others, have succeeded in generating. What matters ultimately is not that Steve Staunton's men will win the European Cup - because nearly everyone agrees that they won't - but that we eventually emerge as good losers and that the national media will mirror that national need to be noticed, for something.

Another limitation of our smallness is that, in Ireland, everyone eventually meets everyone else. In the social columns of our national papers the same people seem to attend the same gatherings and pose for the same pictures, wearing the same smiles and often dressed in the same clothes. But so much of what might be gently mocked or even usefully pilloried - like that sad, tough unintentionally hilarious publication, VIP - will escape our humourous consideration because sooner or later the mocker and the mocked will meet in the bar of the Shelbourne Hotel.

It is no surprise that, despite their Irish provenance, Goldsmith, Sheridan, Wilde and Shaw seem more a part of the English tradition of literary humour. To find home-grown humorists we have to trawl the shallows of modern Irish literature - Hugh Leonard's caustic commentaries on the minutiae of the same Dublin scene and the expletive-sodden Roddy Doyle fables that craven critics have failed to rigorously critique. Or the increasingly strangulated hyperbole of Kevin Myers, riding a series of hobby horses and with a columnist's delightful unawareness of inconsistency. Or viewing reality through the sieve of one's own prejudices - like seeing the Church as a kind of heritage society responsible for the maintenance of listed buildings.

Now that we need humour we realise both the value and the lack of it. Not least in matters religious. Chesterton it was, I think, that champion of Catholic orthodoxy, who suggested that, in the gospels, when Jesus temporarily withdraws from the scene he does so to laugh up his sleeve at the inconsistencies and idiosyncracies of the human condition.

There's a case to be made, at the moment, for the humorous dissecting of our beleaguered Church and a good-humoured mocking of the ambiguities attendant on dragging, comparatively speaking, a Tyrannosaurus Rex into the twenty-first century, the equivalent of giving a drowsy lion a short back and sides. Imagine the possibilites: depressed churchmen talking about joy; a gerontocracy, incapable of even climbing the stairs, wondering why it's out of sync with teenagers; Vatican civil servants agonising over inclusive language in worhsiping and arguing, in effect, that using 'man' in the generic sense might lead to the Armageddon of women's ordination. At the very least, a dollop of humour might help us evade a great deal of pain, frustration and progressive embarrassment of Church allegiance in Ireland today. Our God just has to giggle sometimes.

There's a case to be made too for surfacing the fertile vein of pretensiousness that attends our present prosperity: the gap between making silage and going to the gym, between going to the bog or Marbella, between a midnight scurry to the bottom of the garden and en suite bathrooms; between the way we were and the way we are. Aristotle, once said that the human species is the only animal that laughs. We should treasure the logic of that truth a bit more. To laugh lest we cry. Three cheers for the sanity of humour and a God who giggles.

Old fogies like me often find ourselves shaking our heads in amazement at the turn in Ireland's economic fortunes and the waste of money (as we see it) that is part and parcel of Irish life. But brides and grooms today don't know what we're talking about. What's the big deal? What's €30,000 among friends? Maybe they're right. Such lavish days are what memories are made of

Days of full and plenty

WEDDINGS are, as we say now, something else altogether. And the buoyant industry surrounding them in these days of full and plenty have to be experienced to be believed. A couple, adamant that their big day has to be something special, often seem easy prey to the ever-increasing gallery of wedding service providers lining up to part them from their savings or their borrowings.

Once a wedding was a small morning occasion where close families gathered in a church for Mass and a simple exchange of vows. This was followed by a 'Wedding Breakfast' in one of their homes or later on in a local hotel - the essence of sophistication. Then it was back home to continue the work of the day or in a few cases it meant taking the midday train from Ballina for a few days honeymoon in Dublin and the requisite wedding photograph in a Dublin studio. But for most there were no photographers, no honeymoon.

The only expense, apart from the new clothes, was the fee to the priest, in the past a considerable sum that, we're told, had the priest rubbing his hands in anticipated glee. And priests, no doubt for pastoral reasons, didn't take kindly to other priests being imported into their parishes for the big day. A former PP of Castleconnor in Sligo, not widely acclaimed for the sophistication of his liturgies, once told a young couple who suggested having another priest for their marriage that he had no problem with anyone doing the marriage as long as he got the money!

Now, of course, weddings are hugely complicated affairs. First hotels have to booked at least a year ahead. Hotels now 'specialise' in wedding receptions, which means (in this modern world of consultancies and specialisation) that they can more or less charge what they like for providing a large room, a standard meal and an opportunity to sell mini-oceans of drink at hugely inflated prices – more than anyone could possibly be able or want to consume.

Someone told me recently that the standard wedding meal is now €50 a plate. Hard to believe, isn't it. Or indeed justify. For two hundred people that's €10,000 straight off and that doesn't include a second 'starter', the wine, the obligatory drink for the toast or the other sundries that are now regarded as essential. It always amazes me that hotels, especially wedding hotels seem to be the only retailers who charge top price regardless of the number involved. In any other retail business the more you buy the greater the discount.

After the hotel is booked the preparation period begins in earnest and often it's centred around expectations dumped on couples because of their participation in other couples' weddings. There's a growing list of wedding extras that have become requirements because of peer pressure. Most of them are notoriously expensive which, for some reason that I can't get my head around, makes them all the more important.

Like the Hen Party, when girl friends of the bride gather for a night out, and the Stag Night when their male counterparts do the same. These sessions are now, it seems, a necessary part of the run-up to a wedding. Once they were fairly muted affairs, little more than a few cans of beer and a few ham sandwiches. Now, in our more prosperous and precocious times, they are all night or weekend affairs, and are often overseas - Barcelona, apparently, is the in-place now. Suffice it to say that while they have become obligatory in the wedding process, couples often live to regret them, not just in terms of the expense involved but because when drink flows and defences are down people often say more than they intended and lifelong feuds can ensue.

Then there are a list of other areas to be attended to: the wedding dress, bridesmaids' dresses, groom's suit, bestman's and groomsmen's suits or 'tails', 'going away attire', hair arrangements, music for the church and hotel, flowers for the Church and hotel, getting the rub-on tan just right; the bridal car, the rings, presents for the bridesmaid and best man, bouquets of flowers for the two mothers and/or grandmothers. And the honeymoon – in what used to be Zanzibar.

And if you're getting married and all of that wears you out just thinking about it, there are now wedding consultants who will organise the whole thing for you, for an appropriately gargantuan stipend.

Old fogies like me often find ourselves shaking our heads in amazement at the turn in Ireland's economic fortunes and the waste of money (as we see it) that is part and parcel of Irish life. But brides and grooms today don't know what we're talking about. What's the big deal? What's your problem? Just because their parents couldn't afford a house or if they did took thirty years to furnish it, so what? What's €30,000 among friends? Maybe they're right. Such lavish days are what memories are made of.

Once upon a time, in the good old days, when everything was much simpler, the stipend for the priest cost more than the wedding breakfast. A colleague of mine, who has a great sense of history, feels it a pity that this tradition hasn't continued. Imagine a priest explaining to a couple that his stipend for the day would work out at approximately €10,000! It would be easier to get them to do the pre-marriage course.

The unassailable truth is that the media, like any other public body, cannot be trusted to regulate its own affairs. This principle seems wonderfully appropriate when the media address the limitations of the Church and other public bodies but, for some unknown reason, apparently doesn't apply to the media themselves. Like and all other public institutions, the media too have to accept that, in everyone's interest, they should not and cannot be allowed to regulate themselves.

Time for a press council

Clarify the main point, someone said once, and everything else will fall into place. And the fundamental point about newspapers, for instance, is that they are in the business of making money. That's it.

Yes, I know, get a few hacks together in a small room or late at night or worse still in a radio studio, and they'll conspire to convince you that they're saving the world. A free press will become one of the bulwarks of democracy; keeping the unaccountable accountable will become part of that high moral ground they despise in others but that they themselves inhabit with an arrogant swagger; and the NUJ code of conduct will be taken out and dusted as if it any longer meant anything to anyone. 'Journalistic ethics' has become debased coinage if not an embarrassing oxymoron, a contradiction in terms.

The truth is that, in most Irish newspapers now, there are only two reservations about printing anything: (a) will the law allow it and (b) will our readers accept it.

This reality became abundantly clear in the reporting, for example, of Liam Lawlor's death. *The Sunday Independent* and *The Sunday Tribune*, for example, reported that Lawlor was with a prostitute when he died. It was, of course, untrue but that didn't matter because Lawlor was dead so he couldn't sue. And both editors apologised not, I believe, because they got it wrong but because they quickly realised that their readers wouldn't wear it. What drove the story was money and what drove the apology was money. Grubby hands in a greasy till were all over the story from start to finish.

Because even if the story was true, even if the young woman was a prostitute, journalistic ethics (if such exotic considerations still mattered) would have indicated that, in deference to Lawlor's wife and family, that dimension of the story would not have been published. What was wrong about the story was not that it was untrue, as John Waters pointed out in *The Irish Times*, but that it was published at all.

Commercial considerations drive newspapers. Full stop. An example of that is the present dumbing down of *The Irish Independent*. Several days before *The Ferns Report* was published a series of apparent exclusives revealed all sorts of details about what was in the report. In fact the coverage contained nothing new, apart from re-working stories already in the public forum and combining them with a few intemperate opinion pieces from the usual suspects.

Pretensions to balance or other journalistic standards went out the window and when the report was eventually published, a feature of the *Irish Independent*'s coverage was the employment of short-term contract 'experts' to pen vituperative opinion pieces that inevitably called for the resignation of some bishop or other, the virulence of the language seeking to disguise the limitations of the arguments.

Newspapers now demand that journalists, if that term is not inaccurate, produce commercial copy. In other words, what matters is not whether something is true or even whether it makes any sense but that it helps to sell the paper. So journalists, many of whom are on short-term contracts, write to order just as stringers for national papers search out at local level juicy tit-bits for the nation's tabloids. A media version of the 'no foal, no fee' principle.

Once upon a time there was some discussion about whether we needed a Press Council to regulate the media in Ireland. There's no real question about it now because the reporting of the Lawlor death has given the government the opportunity to do what everyone accepts, apart from the multi-millionaires who control Irish newspapers and those who commercially drive their papers for them, needs to be done.

What we need is an independent statutory body that has the independence, status, power and bottle to regulate Irish media. Of course, those whose job it is to do the dirty work for the media moguls so that they can add another million to their bank balances will be expected to argue against a press council.

The unassailable truth is that the media, like any other public body, cannot be trusted to regulate its own affairs. This principle seems wonderfully appropriate when the media address the limitations of the Church and other public bodies but, for some unknown reason, apparently doesn't apply to the media themselves. Like the Church, the Gardaí, the legal profession and all other public institutions, the media too have to accept that, in everyone's interest, they should not and cannot be allowed to regulate themselves.

If, in the recent criticisms of the Church re *The Ferns Report*, it was taken for granted by the media that any institution that exerts huge influence in society and has been shown to inflict real damage on individuals and families needs an independent agency to keep an eye on its members, then does that same principle not apply to the media?

Maybe then what's sauce for the goose may become sauce for the gander and like bishops, editors and even journalists may well on occasion be asked to do the decent thing and hand in their biros.

A culture of complaint is fuelled by the democratic sense that every opinion is important, even when the person has nothing to say. Guys who never did a day's work in their lives feel obliged to go on Liveline to explain what's wrong with the Irish economy. Someone else who spent two days in hospital knows how to reform the health service

Grumble Ireland

THE old joke comes to mind of the music manager holding auditions for a new pop band. A bunch of youngsters is struggling to impress. Eventually their future manager glares at them and pronounces: *You can't sing, you can't play; you look terrible; you'll be a great success.*

And then there was Eddie Hobbs. Someone, somewhere looking for a silly summer idea for a television programme came up with the notion that they would put Eddie Hobbs standing on a stage in front of an audience talking about the cost of living.

Everything about it is wrong: the jokes were terrible; the insets were uninteresting (for example, Eddie sitting in a car making calls on a mobile phone); the accent grated; Eddie is no Robert Redford; the patter was full of cliches; and the arguments were full of holes.

Yet it worked, at least as television. The third programme had the fourth highest viewership figures of 2006 on RTÉ television. And it worked because *Rip Off Republic* tapped into a vein that media endlessly search out: something that strikes a chord with people, an approach that resonates with an idea they are struggling to articulate themselves. Get someone to say it in a way that makes sense to them and they will watch it forever.

For example, in these critical times for the Catholic church, imagine a cantankerous PP preaching on family life on a cold February Sunday in the back of beyond. He has a bad cold; he didn't sleep very well the night before; nobody is paying him any attention; and a baby is wailing at the back of the Church. Suddenly something snaps, he loses the run of himself, slips into automatic pilot, starts giving out about single parents and, horror of horrors, actually mentions the name of a young woman in the parish.

In the front seat is a journalist, a stringer for the Dublin tabloid press, only there because it's an anniversary Mass for his father and his mother is still alive so he feels he has to be there. Listening to this elderly cleric, rambling on about the woes of the world, he can scarcely believe his luck. Already the tabloid headings and the large fee for a lead story are dancing before his eyes.

The rest, as we say, is history. Gerry Ryan will milk it to his heart's content. That mixture of sex and religion will run for the best part of an hour. *Liveline* will be ringing the parochial house and a sweet little girl will try to charm the charmless Canon into talking to Joe Duffy live on air. You know Canon, she'll say, a lot of people agree with you. It needs to be said. And you should have the chance to put your side of the story. Or if you like, we can record you beforehand and you don't need to be a bit nervous.

That story would run and run. People who had similar experiences would come on *Liveline*, break down crying as they recall the experience, lacerate the Canon and his ilk and go on to talk about everything from the fact that a local curate is driving a new car (and less would have done him) to the scandal of clerical child sexual abuse and who do those people think they are?

A vein had been struck and everyone with a gripe, real or imaginary, against the Catholic Church is sucked into the discussion.

Eddie Hobbs struck a vein too. There is in Ireland a vast and developing culture of complaint, everything from planning permission to the cost of living to the government and the Catholic Church and the County Council and whatever you're having yourself.

That culture of complaint is fuelled by the democratic sense that every opinion is important, even when the person has nothing to say or doesn't make any sense. Guys who never did a day's work in their lives

118

feel obliged to go on *Liveline* to explain what's wrong with the Irish economy. Or if they can't get on *Liveline*, they will bend the ear of whoever happens to sit beside them at a bar counter at 3 o'clock in the afternoon. People who don't want to work will complain about all these foreigners coming into the country taking all the jobs they might look for themselves if the old back wasn't coming again them. Someone who used to go to Mass years ago feels qualified to pontificate on how the Church should get its act together. Someone else who spent two days in hospital knows how to reform the health service (and if Mr Drumm would only listen to them . . .)

These people are not experts. They're wafflers and while it makes good radio and television, it often doesn't make much sense. There are huge gaping holes in Eddie Hobbs's arguments – like, if the government stop taking tax from the motorist, where will they get it? – but what matters in the world of media is not that you make sense but that you press the right buttons. All Eddie Hobbs has to do is confirm the prejudices of his viewers. Just that.

Nobody is going to say the one simple thing that needs to be said: we are a high cost of living economy because people are now earning good wages. Full stop. *Rip Off Ireland* may be good television but it does a disservice to the truth by pretending that there are simple answers to complex questions.

There is a distinction to be made between atheists and what might be termed Irish atheists. Atheists often arrive at a position of non - belief because of intellectual difficulties with belief. Irish atheists, on the other hand, often arrive at a form of non-belief as a reaction to their experience of religious belief.

Crusading athiests

FROM time to time a controversy rages about whether we should have the *Angelus* on radio and television. It's a Catholic prayer, the argument goes, and our public service broadcasting stations shouldn't be seen to favour one denomination. Once that argument is put, someone (usually from another denomination) puts the counter argument that the substance of the prayer (a statement of belief in the Incarnation) is held in common by all Christian faiths. But what about those who are not Christians? The usual response is that the ringing of the *Angelus* Bell is simply a call to prayer for anyone who believes in God. But what about those who don't believe in God?

Atheists too have a right to their place in the sun. Once faith people were very scathing in their approach to those who didn't believe - either agnostics (those who don't know if there's a God) or atheists (those who believe there isn't.) They were dismissed as trouble-makers, reactionaries, ignoramuses. 'Intolerance' wasn't too strong a word for our attitude to them. Nowadays people who have no faith in God, people who are convinced that God doesn't exist, are respected for their beliefs or non-beliefs. Atheism is, in that sense, a respectable world-view.

But times have changed. And just as once believers attacked and ridiculed atheists for their non-beliefs, now you often find atheists ridiculing believers for their beliefs. And intolerance isn't too strong a word for that either.

There is too, I think, a distinction to be made between atheists and what might be termed *Irish* atheists. Atheists often arrive at a position of non-belief because of intellectual difficulties with belief. *Irish* atheists, on the other hand, often arrive at a form of non-belief as a reaction to their *experience* of religious belief.

For some people, for example, the word 'Catholic' is a synonym for oppression. Their experience of what the atheist Richard Dawkins calls 'the closed, authoritarian, faith-based beliefs of revealed religion' has turned them off God. Over-religious parents, over-zealous teachers and over-pious priests created the impression that belief in God comes through a narrow funnel that doesn't allow for reason or intelligence.

The experience of religion is so cloyed, so narrow, so oppressive that the first chance they get they run away from it. And to justify their abandonment of the God their parents believed in, they need to present religion as something associated with control, ignorance and superstition.

Scratch an Irish atheist and you often find that his atheism is only skin-deep. He'll talk about the sexual abuse of children by priests and religious, the Magdalen laundries, the domination of Irish life by the Catholic Church, how fond priests were (or are) of money, the Crusades, the Inquisition, the Popes in the sixteenth century.

He won't accept or even note all that is good in the history and tradition of the Catholic faith: that for every Inquisitor there was a Francis of Assisi; for every abusing or bullying or ignorant priest there are ninety others who treat their parishioners with respect and care; that for every abusive or violent nun there were ninety others who gave exceptional service to the poorest of the poor; for every oppressed and oppressing believer there were others who opened hearts and minds to the richness that religious faith can bring.

Scratch an Irish atheist and you may find someone who had religion forced down his throat, someone for whom belief in a Catholic God became a weight he had to get out from under in order to survive as a human being, someone who came to presume that reason and intelligence sat awkwardly with religious faith, someone who was taught that sex could be equated with sin.

Other Irish atheists are those who have had 'normal' religious upbringing but who resent the Church telling people what to do. There's an ethos emerging that can be dismissed as 'individualism' but is in effect a result, I believe, of people having the confidence to make up their minds for themselves and to own their own truths. What often pushes people away from the Church, even away from religious belief, is the failure of the Church to listen to and trust the faith experience of such people. (It's also a failure of theology, but that's another question.) Instead of engaging with intelligence and reason, the Church ends up demanding assent, throwing its weight, dismissing debate and pushing people searching for a spiritual sense away from religious belief.

Finally there are the anti-religious, crusading atheists - people like Richard Dawkins who see religious faith as a contagious virus. And just as in the past religious zealots denounced heresies, there are now anti-religious zealots ridiculing any form of belief as unscientific, old-fashioned, out of date.

Dawkins, for instance, in a recent book wrote a moving letter to his young daughter advocating the joys of clear-thinking (i.e non-religious) yet is scathing of the fact, in *The Selfish Gene*, that 'it is a telling fact that, the world over, the vast majority of children follow the religion of their parents.' Isn't that what parents are supposed to do, advise their children. As, it is clear, he too wants to do.

The fact is that atheism is itself a belief system. And if it becomes popular, we'll have to have an 'Angelus Bell' for atheists too, to give them the chance to reflect on their non-belief in God.

Older priests are notoriously susceptible to being persuaded that (i) the Church can't do without them and (ii) that their present parish would fall apart at the seams if they weren't there. The more difficult truth is that it is good for a diocese to have a definite retirement policy; that it is good for the parish when a priest retires; and that it is good for the priest himself. Retirement, properly managed and prepared for, can be a blessing for everyone involved.

Retiring priests

THERE'S an old joke about a parish priest in America. One Sunday morning, on his 95th birthday, he informed his parishioners that the bishop had prevailed on him to accept another five-year extension. 'So it's my privilege and duty to continue as your pastor here - as well as being pastor of St Michael's, St Monica's, St Philip's, St John the Baptist's, St Peter's . . .'

We have problems with retirement. Most Irish priests retire at 75, some quite relieved, others under duress. In some dioceses retirement happens at 70. In individual cases some priests resign their parishes at 70 or 65 or in a few cases 60 and opt for a less demanding though full-time position. Others due to ill-health choose other options. Even though, in today's world, retiring at 75 seems somewhat antediluvian even bizarre the fluidity of the system probably suits our tradition and our temperament. At least up to now.

But as the age-level of priests increases and a significant scarcity of priests kicks in the need for a less *ad hoc* approach to retirement is needed. In a few years there will be significantly fewer priests in Ireland and coupled with an incomprehensible lack of planning for this all-too-predictable scenario the likelihood is that many priests who should be retiring will be pressured to keep working.

A few years ago an American bishop wrote a letter to his 'Senior' priests. Clearly the letter was designed to encourage as many priests as possible to continue in ministry.

All the predictable buttons were pressed: (i) priests are not 'of this world' so shouldn't be enticed into blindly following their secular counterparts; (ii) "the holy priesthood is not a career"; (iii) a financial inducement; (iv) an appeal to vanity – 'In some instances, when it is judged appropriate by both the priest and bishop, the honorary title of Pastor Emeritus may be conferred'; (v) 'the Church needs you'; (vi) many priests find retirement disappointing; and, (vii), believe it or not, 'Moses was already an old man when the Lord gave him the mission to lead the chosen people out of Egypt – what if he had said *No, Lord, I am retired*?'

Even though the bishop mentioned that those who seek retirement should be free to accept it with 'an unburdened conscience', that latter point was less than prominent in his letter. The main gist of it was that any priest in good health should continue working.

I would imagine that I'm not alone in finding that approach to the retirement of priests unfair, disrespectful and patently manipulative. If a priest has served 40 or 45 or 50 years in active ministry, he deserves to be encouraged into retirement rather than made to feel guilty if he seeks to enjoy life in the few years God may give him. (Or alternatively not indulged in an unthinking decision to keep going.) He may well offer his services in some auxiliary ministry but it should be by his choice and on his own terms. And from a position of official retirement.

Older priests are notoriously susceptible to being persuaded that (i) the Church can't do without them and (ii) that their present parish would fall apart at the seams if they weren't there. The more difficult truth is that it is good for a diocese to have a definite retirement policy; that it is good for the parish when a priest retires; and that it is good for the priest himself. Retirement, properly managed and prepared for, can be a blessing for everyone involved.

Part of the problem is the old 'die in harness' syndrome. Priests were ordained never to retire and thus enforced retirement is experienced as akin to a death. Nobody wants me. Nobody gives me any attention. Nobody values the work I've done. This underlines the need to prepare early on for retirement and to begin to address this need while priests are still active and healthy. And less susceptible to that definitive clerical whining exacerbated by the onset of old age.

At least as early as our fifties (when most of our counterparts in lay life are *de facto* retiring) we should be encouraged to begin reflecting on our future retirements, to attend courses, to understand what the possibilities are and on. A diocesan policy should encourage a gradual disengagement: first, from administrative duties; then, from the position of PP; later, from key responsibilities, facilitating an acceptance of a decline in status (God help us all); and eventually, easing into full retirement, and - depending on health, energy and competence - choosing some manageable auxiliary ministry.

A diocesan retirement strategy would allow decisions to be made not suddenly at 75 but gradually over the previous twenty years. Arrangements regarding housing should be clearly set out. Policy should be defined. For example, the wisdom of PPs not retiring in either the parish or the parochial house. And so on.

It's all part of the importance of active, responsible retirement today. Priests have a lot to learn from the wider society about humane and sensible ways of managing the end of our lives. Active preparation for retirement is an important part of that: developing hobbies, 'letting go', deciding where you want to live, maintaining important and significant friendships. And accepting that old age brings with it not just wisdom but a gradual and debilitating inability to make decisions and to manage our lives. Especially as we often make such decisions on our own.

Retirement for priests is a right which should be generously and respectfully taken for granted.

Surely the least we might expect is that even a few of the thousands and thousands of people who, without the Church, might not have had an education at all, might raise their voices to balance the present argument. Where are the Blackrock boys now? And the St Muredach's lads and the St Jarlath's celebrated alumni?

One solitary voice

THE *Letter of the Week* in *The Western People* came to the defence of the Catholic Church. From a 29 year-old who described himself as 'not a saintly person' it argued, clearly and trenchantly, against the present feeding frenzy on the Catholic Church and its clergy.

The letter made some important distinctions: for example, between God and the Catholic Church, between individual clergy and the great majority of clergy. It was the kind of letter that, in the present troubles afflicting the Catholic Church, might be regularly expected from concerned, literate lay-people. There was just one problem with this letter: the person who wrote it didn't sign his or her name.

While I regret that anonymity I can understand it. Who now publicly wants to stand up for the Catholic Church and for Catholic priests and religious in Ireland? Apart from the odd Church of Ireland rector, nobody. In the present climate erstwhile supporters are keeping their counsel. And from those who benefitted directly from the contribution of the Church in the past to education, to poverty programmes and so on the silence is deafening.

The Catholic Church in Ireland is the whipping boy of the present time. Savage the Catholic church now and hardly anyone will raise a flag in its defence. Once when passions were running high in the North and anti-British and anti-unionist feelings were the order of the day, you still found people walking out of Wolfe Tones concerts in protest against their undiluted support for the Provos. But attend a Des Bishop or Tommy Tiernan concert and the Catholic Church and its adherents are hung, drawn and quartered to the apparent delight of packed audiences.

And even the politicians, trying to establish (or re-establish) reputations, have discovered in the Catholic Church the softest of soft targets. Once politicians collected votes by licking up to the Church, now with their unerring ability of keeping their fingers on the popular pulse they sense that there are more votes to be harvested from kicking the Church than praising it.

One source of criticism directed at the Catholic Church is, what the media describe as, the 'sweetheart deal' Michael Woods achieved for the Church in terms of the percentage religious orders will have to pay to survivors of abuse in industrial homes in relation to the State's contribution. The ratio should be fifty-fifty, the argument goes, rather than the third or even quarter, depending on how the overall figures eventually will pan out. The Catholic Church, the argument goes, should pay its fair share.

Its fair share? But what is a fair share? When we quantify the contributions the state and the Catholic Church have made to a whole range of areas in Irish life, should we not be quantifying everything church-people do?

An example. Recently I had a letter from the Marriage Registration office, enclosing a number of forms which apparently some civil servants wish me to hand out on their behalf to couples getting married. (The civil registration of marriage requires giving three months notice to the state and the office dealing with the administration of this requirement has introduced a new form.) The accompanying letter informed me that I could give out the new forms. Or I could photo-copy them, if I ran out. Or I could take them down from their web-site. Whatever I liked.

I could, on the other hand, put them back into the envelope and post them - without a stamp! - back to the civil servant who dumped them on me (and, presumably, thousands of priests around the country) and tell him to give them out himself.

Let me let you in on a secret. I'm fed up being an unpaid civil servant. And I suspect that thousands of my colleagues are of the same view. Include in that the management of primary schools since the foundation of the state. Include in it too the fund-raising efforts to provide resources for schools when the state couldn't or wouldn't provide them. Include in it all the meetings attended, all the interventions in all the disputes, all the cajoling and all the encouraging of voluntary efforts at local level so that the work of the state could be subsidised by the unpaid labour of priests and religious. You couldn't possibly list it all, if you had acres of paper. And if you could achieve a balance sheet at the end of it, who owes whom, the state or the Church?

When it suits the state to take advantage of our unpaid labour, no one has any problem at all. But if we're assessing what's due to whom I think, in truth and in justice, the Catholic Church, for all its failures (and they are many) should expect a fairer wind.

Surely the least we might expect is that even a few of the thousands and thousands of people who, without the Church, might not have had an education at all, might raise their voices to balance the present argument. Where are the Blackrock boys now? And the St Muredach's lads and the St Jarlath's celebrated alumni?

And surely the least we might expect from the thousands and thousands of families who were kept body and soul together by the resources of the church, surely there's a son or daughter somewhere who might find a voice to speak the truth?

Or has the Catholic Church to depend on a solitary, anonymous voice in a local paper?

At local level, the drift away from regular worship is creating a new generation of nominal Catholics whose knowledge of their faith and the rituals that sustain it are becoming more and more ephemeral. Add to that the incoming tide of this great secular age and the excesses of our Tiger economy and what you get is a generation in the process of forgetting the Christian story. The challenge now is: how do we tell and re-tell the Christian story in an age when it is slipping from memory.

Retelling the story

IN a previous existence I used to attend the county convention of Sligo GAA. Usually it was a long and, I often felt, unnecessarily drawn-out and tedious experience where worthy but dull homilies were addressed to the assembled Gaels. However, as a refugee from my native Mayo I was always taken by the belief, even passion, that was evident every year that, regardless of the evidence, 'this would be Sligo's year'. Every convention ended with the hope that Sligo would make it to Croke Park on the third Sunday of September.

We all knew that Sligo had never won a senior All-Ireland. We all knew that the possibilities, then as now unfortunately, seemed very limited. We all knew that it was a long, long road from here to there. But, despite all of that, every year the convention sponsored a series of impassioned speeches geared to inflame the expectations of even the more realistic supporters of Sligo football. The dream lived on.

I thought of Sligo GAA conventions when I heard the Chief Rabbi of England, Jonathan Sacks on BBC Radio 4's *Thought for the Day* on the sixtieth anniversary of the liberation of the Bergen-Belsen concentration camp. Sacks posed the question for himself: 'How did Jews survive all these centuries of persecution . . . why didn't they just give up?' The answer he came up with was: 'We never forgot the story;

we taught it to our children and we always told it in such a way as to end on a note of hope: this year we are slaves, next year we'll be free.' The story was the Passover, the story of God's care for the Jews. It was the telling and re-telling of the story of the Passover that kept hope alive.

I don't intend any disrespect to the suffering of the Jewish people when I use that story of enduring hope to understand why Sligo football needs to tell and retell its own story, to keep hope alive. I use it rather to illustrate the need for the Christian Churches to find ways to continue telling our story because unless we find new ways then the story and the memory that sustained it will slip into oblivion.

Once the story told itself because it was carried along on a current of political and social action. In the past, for example, Catholic identity was part of a confused mix of Irishness, colonisation, inequality, anti-Englishness, anti-Protestantism, anti-landlordism and so on. The Catholic bit was just part of a great river, the different elements of which kept the current flowing.

Now, in a sense, the Catholic thing has run aground. In the upper echelons, Catholicism is now often regarded as something of an embarrassment, its excesses dismissed as remnants of a by-gone age. In the media, Catholicism is a convenient and soft target to be attacked at will by hacks anxious to advertise their liberal credentials.

At local level, the drift away from regular worship is creating a new generation of nominal Catholics whose knowledge of their faith and the rituals that sustain it are becoming more and more ephemeral. Add to that the incoming tide of this great secular age and the excesses of our Tiger economy and what you get is a generation in the process of forgetting the Christian story. The challenge now is: how do we tell and re-tell the Christian story in an age when it is slipping from memory.

Because no matter how much money we have or what level of lifestyle we enjoy, sooner or later we are confronted with the deeper questions. Someone we love is dead; or a child is seriously ill; or a relationship that sustained us falls apart; or a family conflict devastates us; and we begin to see how flimsy and ethereal are money or success or influence.

Sooner or later we begin to ask: what's it all about? what's my life for? what's ultimately satisfying? What does it all mean? And we find that an extra holiday in the sun or yet another extension to the home or a bigger car or a new obsession about our weight or whatever are about as useful as a pile of dust. When the big questions come to visit us in the small hours they demand our respect and attention.

And if we have no context for them, if all we can come up with for understanding our place in the great scheme of things is some worthy goal (like caring the planet) we end up not giving such important questions our respectful attention and the only anti-dote is to distract ourselves with technology or whatever.

But the fundamental questions won't go away, you know. And to give them our respectful attention, we need to situate them in some kind of faith-context. Which is why telling and re-telling the Christian story is so important. Because if we forget the story, if it drifts away to the edges of life, then we end up listening to the echoes of the loudest voices.

If God is moved to the margins of our lives, out of sight and often out of mind, is it any wonder that so many today no longer know the words. Which is why, like the Jews and the Passover, and the Sligo GAA dreaming about Croke Park on a September Sunday, we need to keep telling and re-telling the Christian story.

What brought that seismic change were things like education, travel, television, technology, prosperity and the resultant mix brought different perspectives on life: a greater emphasis on personal freedom; a more, open and inclusive and tolerant approach to life. But there was a downside too: a loss of respect; the decline of community, even neighbourliness; a growing emphasis on acquiring things; a greed for money and property; a loss of ordinary decency; a loss of respect for the wisdom of the old.

Different Irelands

As part of a history project on priests of Killala diocese I've been trawling through back issues of the *Western People*, courtesy of Castlebar Library, a huge resource centre for history buffs and with a startlingly impressive ambiance, both personal and professional. Lately I've been delving into the 1940s.

At the time *Western People* readers were being told by advertisers that *Andrews Liver Salt* refreshes and purifies, that *Robin Starch* gives wings to your iron, *Cuticura Ointment* was the prescribed anti-dote to septic poisoning and if you had a stuffed nose or a sore throat or a tight chest all you had to do was rub on Vick. And on Friday, 29th September 1944, Johnny Weissmuller and Maureen O'Sullivan were starring in *Tarzan's New York Adventure* in the Estoria Cinema in Ballina.

Earlier in that same year, 1944, Bishop James Naughton, in his Lenten Pastoral, reminded the people of the diocese of Killala, that dances were strictly forbidden during the whole of Lent as were all public entertainments not in keeping with 'the penitential spirit of the holy season.' And that they should also remember that throughout the year 'dances are strictly prohibited on all Saturdays and on the eves of holydays of obligation.'

In the issue of July 13th 1940, Canon Michael Tully of Easkey called on the government to proscribe foreign dances and jazz music, by law if necessary, in the interests of both the physical and moral well-being of young people. 'Too much freedom,' Canon Tully said, at the opening of Easkey Feis, 'has been allowed to people in these matters'.

It seems another world and it is. God only knows what Bishop Naughton and Canon Tully would think of Bono and U2 strutting their stuff in Croke Park, of all places. All that strange music, encouraging all those foreign dances, all that freedom. Croke Park, that bastion of all things Irish: Irish games, Irish language, Irish traditions. How, Canon Michael Tully would surely say, how has it all come to this? And Bishop Naughton would nod sadly in agreement.

What brought that seismic change were things like education, travel, television, technology, prosperity and the resultant mix brought different perspectives on life: a greater emphasis on personal freedom; a more, open and inclusive and tolerant approach to life.

But there was a downside too: a loss of respect; the decline of community, even neighbourliness; a growing emphasis on acquiring things; a greed for money and property; a loss of ordinary decency; a loss of respect for the wisdom of the old.

But having said all that, and even though the elderly often pine for the simplicity and maybe the piety of the past, I don't think too many of us would want to go back to where we were. Whatever our reservations about the way the world is now, in a referendum I think Bono's Ireland would get a lot more support than Canon Tully's Ireland.

But despite the difference, some things don't change. Like human nature. Or the big questions that pickle every life : what's my life for? what does it all mean? what happens when we die? where is God in all this? Or the need to make sense of it all. Or, in other words, the challenge to place our lives in a faith context.

Canon Tully's Ireland was a place where speaking Irish was better than speaking English, Irish dancing was better than foreign dancing, Irish music was better than jazz, Catholics were better than Protestants, playing Gaelic football was better than soccer.

Bono and U2 represent, in a way, a new and different Ireland, an Ireland that's proudly taking it's place in an ever-developing and technological world, a more confident Ireland, a more tolerant Ireland, a more inclusive Ireland, an Ireland where at long last people are paid decent wages for decent work. And thank God for it.

We may not be, as a country, all that we might be. We may sometimes be tempted, in our rush for the new, to neglect the wisdom of the old. But Bono the Irishman, leading the most popular band in the world, on a huge stage on the sacred soil of Croke Park represents a new and very different Ireland.

Those of us who remember the two Irelands have to pinch ourselves sometimes to ensure what has happened isn't just a dream or a nightmare, depending on your perspective. But for those who grew up in Bono's Ireland, the comparison is academic. *Robin Starch* or *Cuticura Ointment* or even *Vick* are no longer on their radar. And they haven't a clue who Johnny Weissmuller and Maureen O'Sullivan were. The 1940s are past history. Citizens of Bono's brave new world world don't even know what we're talking about.

The whole thrust of the Second Vatican Council was that the Catholic Church would become a people's Church, that people would accept the duty of exercising their gifts in the service of the gospel. But how can this be done if the structures necessary to facilitate the exercise of those gifts are not put in place? How can we become a people's Church if the clerical Church will not listen?

Picking and choosing

IN recent years the disparaging phrase '*a la carte* Catholicism' has become common place. It refers to the tendency (some people are reputed to have) of 'picking and mixing' their Catholic faith. If I like this bit I'll take it; if I don't like this other bit, I'll ignore it. As if the Catholic faith was like a box of *Irish Rose,* where you thumb around to get your favourite sweet and the uninteresting and unpopular ones are left in the bottom of the box. So helping the poor is okay but the Church's teaching on birth-control, well, not too sure about that!

This kind of picking and choosing gets up the noses of some strict Catholics who see it as a way of, in effect, diluting the Catholic faith. They loudly proclaim it as wrong-headed, unacceptable, selfish, heretical and whatever other disparaging epithet rolls off the tongue.

But interestingly some of those who disparage what they call *a-la-carte* Catholicism commit the very sins they accuse other less authentic Catholics of committing. Recently there was a discussion about this very issue in a gathering of clergy and laity at which a very important clergyman - a legend in his own mind – excoriated the compromises of modern Catholics.

Eventually a small still voice asked the gathering if anyone present, who regarded themselves as living the Catholic faith in its fullness, might raise their hands. No one in the room raised a hand, even our orthodox friend, who apparently (as was well known to the group) has left a trail of disaster after him in a series of parishes.

The truth is that no one, apart from the occasional saint, is capable of living the fullness of the Christian faith. The truth is that, in that sense, everyone is an *a-la-carte* Catholic. We know what the ideal is; we understand the various teachings of the Church; we want to live as well as we can; but as fallible and weak individuals we end up, as St Paul famously explained, often doing the very things that we believe we shouldn't be doing; and vice-versa.

Everyone does that. Even great churchmen. Picking and choosing bits of the Catholic faith isn't confined to the more obvious sinners. For instance, in the last forty years, one particular form of *a-la-carte* Catholicism has been practised by the clerical leadership of the Church.

Forty years ago next month, the last great decree of the Second Vatican Council, *The Church in the Modern World*, was issued. What this decree taught was that the Catholic Church needed to regard the world in a positive way and needed to engage with it if the gospel message was to be preached. Who will forget, for example, that hopeful and optimistic call: 'The joys and hopes, the griefs and the anxieties of the people of this age, especially those who are poor or in any way afflicted, these are the joys and hopes, the griefs and anxieties of the followers of Christ.' The Church of the future was no longer to be regarded as a great fortress surrounded by a vast spiritual wilderness but a positive and a good place with which we (as a Church) needed to converse.

But the implications of the decree were soon compromised by the growing fashion in conservative circles to denigrate it. Cardinal Joseph Ratzinger, now Pope Benedict XVI, often showed his distaste for it but as Pope hasn't sustained that position which, in the words of one recent commentator, upholds 'the notion that Catholics may choose to ignore parts of the Church's teaching they find disagreeable.' The Pope can't be an *a-la-carte* Catholic!

Whatever about Benedict XVI, the clerical Church had no problem ignoring this document and even the law of the Church, enshrined in the new Code of Canon Law, which gave some of it substance. For example, how many dioceses, how many parishes, are not in conformity with the requirements of Canon 511 of the Catholic Church's Code of Canon Law? Canon 511 states: 'In each diocese, in so far as pastoral circumstances suggest, a pastoral council is to be established.'

The whole thrust of the Second Vatican Council was that the Catholic Church would become a people's Church, that people would accept the duty of exercising their gifts in the service of the gospel. But how can this be done if the structures necessary to facilitate the exercise of those gifts are not put in place? How can we become a people's Church if the clerical Church will not listen?

Forty years after *The Church in the Modern World* there are still parishes, dioceses even, that have made little or no attempt to put in place basic structures that are not just the official teaching of the Church but essential if the Church is to continue to engage with the modern world. Or even with itself.

It is clear now that there has been, in the forty years since Vatican Two, a systematic failure to introduce Parish Councils, Diocesan Councils, Parish Finance Councils, etc. In some cases bishops and priests have resisted any and every effort to put any such structures in place. And what is particularly galling is that some of them are ever ready to dismiss others as picking and choosing their own version of Catholicism.

So how are things in your parish or diocese, forty years after *The Church in the Modern World?*

Many priests stood at their pulpits the weekend after the RTE Primetime programme, Cardinal Sins, and wondered what their people were thinking about them. Many hadn't the confidence or the skill to address their people's fears or their own sense of betrayal and they ended up saying nothing.

Who cares who's caring for priests?

IT'S no secret that many clergy and religious are in the dumps of despair. It is as if the firm foundations under their feet have shaken; buildings have crumbled around them; and the work of a lifetime lies in the dust before them. How could it all have come to this?

It's bad enough that fewer people are going to Mass, that vocations have almost disappeared, that in a very different Ireland they feel taken for granted or patronised or even regarded as figures of fun.

But now with the clerical child sexual cases and the failure to deal with them, credibility is damaged, authority is diminished, a desolate landscape stretches out before them. Once they were on pedestals; then they were shuffled off them, now they don't really matter, apart from the occasional functional or honorary role on the sidelines. Their world has imploded. No wonder that some of them are heading for the hills.

Those who stay don't quite know what to do. There's an eerie silence or vacuum that many priests are waiting for someone to fill while at the same time sensing that no one quite knows who or what might fill it. Work goes on; the daily grind of pastoral care brings its own momentum; respect is earned at a personal level; but there is evidence of a paralysing unease and unhappiness among priests as they try to work out what has happened to their world.

There's anger among priests too. Anger that the leadership of the Church is ineffective, incompetent and even sometimes non-existent. Some bishops seem to be living in a world of their own imagining. Others seem to believe that they are infallible – even though there's very little evidence to support that thesis. Terrible mistakes have been made. And there seems to be almost a constitutional inability to admit the mistakes, to accept responsibility for them and to learn from the experience. And that failure of leadership is percolating down into parish life, distressing priests, undermining their confidence, diminishing their status, damaging their relationship with their people.

There is too among priests a growing sense of desolation as they see no end to the publicity surrounding the scandals and little prospect of the Church dealing competently with the fall-out from them. They sense they are being left on their own and many feel they haven't the personal or organisational resources to cope.

Many priests stood at their pulpits the weekend after the RTE *Primetime* programme, *Cardinal Sins*, and wondered what their people were thinking about them. Many hadn't the confidence or the skill to address their people's fears or their own sense of betrayal and they ended up saying nothing.

Exacerbating their sense of unease and desolation was the failure of people to support them or to understand how isolated and discomfited they were. When priests die or move to other parishes the ritual tributes can be fulsome but returning to their empty presbyteries that weekend was, for many, a lonely and desolate experience. Some received a few phone-calls of support; for others, the sound of silence felt distinctly ominous.

For more, it underpinned their sense of being regarded as useful functionaries at parish level but without any real sense of community or family support when the going gets rough. Some felt that the anger of people was being directed (unfairly) at the most accessible representative of the Church, the local priest.

Who will speak out for priests? Bishops no longer have a credible voice in that regard. If priests speak themselves it will be dismissed as self-serving. And, reaping the whirlwind of our failure as a church to give our people their rightful place, there are no lay people in positions of significance to confront unfair comment or to defend or support the individual priest working away at parish level.

I spoke recently to a PP who had worked for more than 40 years in his diocese. He wanted to retire, not because he felt he had nothing to contribute, but because he felt discouraged and disillusioned by the leadership of his Church and by the lack of support of his people.

All the work that priests and religious had put into education, all the salaries pumped back into schools, all the extra curricular activities to give children from deprived backgrounds an opportunity to be educated, all the investment in boarding schools for the children of the rich and the middle-classes - and they just took it and walked away, without any sense of the mountain of work put into it or even a suggestion that a word of gratitude might be appropriate.

All the efforts at parish level to build churches, to resource schools, to develop community, to support the elderly, to encourage the young, all the meetings over all the years, all the support for people in distress, all the hidden support of people in abject need - and at the end of the day who cares. People just take it all for granted and priests and religious are left feeling empty and dejected. We've heard the negative stories of abuse and no one would say that they shouldn't be told. Of course they should. But where are the other stories? The ninety-nine others, where are they?

No wonder priests and religious feel used and rejected. No wonder so few young men and women want to follow in our footsteps. No wonder so many priests and are now walking away. Because when the chips are down they are left with the question - who cares for our priests? - and no one, it seems, wants to be part of the answer.

The best letters of all are those written in longhand. A typed letter, no matter how personal, has a formality and a coldness attached to it. It hasn't the natural flow of speech that you identify with the writer . And the letters that we truly treasure are those that carry messages that can be read between the written lines, those that bear the lilt of the voice and the imprint of the personality.

The fading art of letter-writing

It came as something of a shock to me recently to realise that I started writing my column in *The Western People* twenty-seven years ago. It started when I was in Dromard in Sligo. At the beginning I wrote it out studiously in long-hand and then typed it on my Brother baby-typewriter and posted it to Ballina. It was then re-typed in *The Western People*, reproduced in bromide form and placed on a page. The whole process, I remember, played havoc with deadlines. Now nearly a quarter of a century later I type it directly on to a computer and email it directly to the *Western* where it is poured electronically on to this page.

Electronic mail is truly a Godsend. Practically instantaneous communication around the world. And for the price of a local call. People use it all the time: searching for their roots, prospective brides checking their wedding arrangements, emigrants making contact - all part of the very varied uses of email today. A few years ago it was an exotic form of communication: now we just take it for granted.

But despite the ease and usefulness of electronic mail, it's hard to see it replacing the traditional post. There's no comparing the emails tumbling into the inbox on the computer screen with the postman handing you a bundle of letters. The reason of course is that the traditional post has a history and texture to it that electronic mail will never challenge.

There's an excitement about holding a letter in your hand, looking at the writing, deciphering the post-mark, undoing the seal, unfolding the letter, flicking back the pages to find the signature at the end. There's the way too we have of slotting them into compartments: the formal brown envelope that is as dull as its predictable contents; the ones with the little windows in them that contain the bills ; the flashy junk-mail that we casually transfer to the waste basket; the abusive ones that invariably end with 'yours respectfully'; the official long white envelopes that are usually work-related; and then the ordinary letters that we savour, leaving them until last like a luscious dessert.

Opening the post is a ritual hallowed by time. And it has a history behind it: the important letter that came bearing the good or bad tidings, significant moments etched forever into an individual or family consciousness. Or the letter that never came. And the waiting. The first letter from the emigrant son or daughter in England or America. The regular letter with the dollars or the sterling that helped to keep families afloat. And the last letter . . . was it June three years ago and no word since. Maybe this Christmas. All the emotional and personal weight that the letters of our lives have carried over the years!

The best letters of all are those written in longhand. A typed letter, no matter how personal, has a formality and a coldness attached to it. It hasn't the natural flow of speech that you identify with the writer. Longhand has a reality and an authenticity to it - somehow there's more of the person in it. Type is more studied, less personal, more clinical. Typefaces flatten the words, the flow, even the personality. And the letters that we truly treasure are those that carry messages that can be read between the written lines, those that bear the lilt of the voice and the imprint of the personality.

The problem is that fewer of us actually take the time to write the kind of letters that we enjoy receiving. Email or a phone call in response is easier and more immediate. Other letters we leave aside and we promise ourselves to reply to them in kind but often they tend to build into a reproachful pile on a desk, gradually shifted out of sight and sometimes out of mind, until the great clean-out when we end up reassuring myself that it is too late or too embarrassing to respond.

Once letter-writing was a past-time, an art, even a passion. But now we are easily seduced by the telephone and the email and the text messages as the complicated accoutrements of letter-writing - pen, letter, envelope, stamp, even the journey to the post office - conspire to defeat us. Now if we feel compelled to write in longhand we are embarrassed by the unpractised scrawl that we see appearing on the page in front of us. Moreover we have lost the fluidity of thought when the pen was almost an extension of the arm and we find ourselves defeated by the formal letter that would read well in type but looks incongruous and stilted in longhand.

No doubt, electronic mail will become even more popular but there will always be a letter we need to write that is important enough to write in longhand. Because there are some things in life that are too personal and too special to submit to the coldness of type. And the experience of waiting on the post, holding that letter expectantly in your hand and greedily opening it is part of the history of every life.

The debate about women's ordination as priests and bishops within Anglicanism is like a dress rehearsal for the same debate within Catholicism. The cut and thrust of such debate is Anglicanism's gift to the Christian Church in that Anglicanism's tradition of democratic structures and dispersed authority widens the issue beyond the narrower confines of Catholicism's traditions. In Anglicanism it is easier to open up debate: in Catholicism it is easier to close it down.

Long slow burn

Over ten years ago the Church of England decided to ordain women to the priesthood. Part of the fall-out from that decision was the not-unrelated decision of a significant number of Anglican priests and laity to 'convert' to Roman Catholicism.

While no doubt some individuals within that particular movement (from the Church of England to the R.C. Church) based their decision on intellectual conviction the general feeling was that formerly contentious matters like transubstantiation and papal infallibility seemed less important than the inability to stomach the ordination of women.

It seemed as if a re-alignment was taking place: those for or against the ordination of women. The *Fors* stayed with the Church of England : the *Againsts* moved into the Catholic Church. The shift would make it easier for the Church of England to facilitate the ordination of women as priests and, logically, as bishops: and the corresponding resistance to the ordination of women in the R.C. Church was similarly strengthened.

Curiously though, during the summer, an authoritative survey of opinion among CofE clergy threw up the extraordinary statistic that a quarter of them believed that there 'should not be any women bishops ordained anywhere.'

So despite the fact that around four-hundred Anglican clergy had walked away from the CofE in protest against the ordination of women a decade or so ago, a quarter of those remaining don't want to accept the logic of the decision to ordain women as priests, which is to ordain women as bishops. Why is the ordination of women as bishops a bridge too far for one in four CofE clergy? Clearly unease with the ordination of women is a continuing factor.

It's hard to understand the arguments against women priests. Tradition is clearly important but so much of it was socially-conditioned. When Christianity made great strides, it did so by rolling with the cultural norms of the day and that meant that the subservient role of women in society was reflected in the church. Another strand is the culture of revulsion because of the biological functions of the female body. Another is the sense that somehow women hadn't the natural authority of men that is an important constituent of presiding at the altar.

Any one of the above arguments would be difficult to justify today. Christianity has to make its peace with the norms of today's society and that means accepting women as equal partners. The Old Testament notion that women are somehow unclean because of their biological functions makes no sense today. And the so-called lesser authority of women doesn't make any sense in a world where women are prime ministers, airline pilots, surgeons and holders of All Ireland medals.

Interestingly, in the survey quoted above, two thirds of laity are in favour of ordaining women as bishops. And fewer people are opposed to women bishops than were opposed to women priests a decade ago. So despite a rump that looks back to the past the ordination of women as bishops has the force of history running with it.

Where that leaves the Roman Catholic church is another question. In a sense the debate about women's ordination as priests and bishops within Anglicanism is like a dress rehearsal for the same debate within Catholicism. The cut and thrust of such debate is Anglicanism's gift to the Christian Church in that Anglicanism's tradition of democratic structures and dispersed authority widens the issue beyond the narrower confines of Catholicism's traditions. In Anglicanism it is easier to open up debate: in Catholicism it is easier to close it down.

There is a tide in history and if you don't take it you run the risk of being left on the shore. Democracy is part of that tide. The equal status of women in society is another. Yet another is that the gifts of the whole community have to be cherished if the fullness of life and the wholeness of truth is to emerge.

The ordination of women in the Anglican tradition is a headline for Catholicism and the debates it generated have helped to clarify important issues for Roman Catholicism. As the debate about the ordination of women bishops progresses with significant reservation it reflects the long slow burn that is the issue of women priests in Catholicism. *Yes but not yet* to women bishops in the Church of Ireland, a hesitant *Yes but not yet* to women priests in the Roman Catholic Church.

There's something about a cemetery in November. Walking through the graves, reading the headstones, allowing the memories to surface somehow we feel reassured about who we are and what we believe. Nowhere are we closer to our own roots than walking in our own graveyard. To avoid the experience is to avoid our memories. To forget them is to lose track of ourselves.

The leaves of November

W E'RE good at funerals. We're good at paying our respects to the dead. We recognise too how important it is to give moral support to the bereaved. And we still turn out in quite extraordinary numbers. No wonder the *Death Notices* on *Mid West Radio* has the highest listenership of the day. It fits in with the feel for the rituals of death and burial that are thankfully still part of our changing culture. And our feel for November is still very sure. It is still part of what we are as a people. The Holy Souls have this part of the Christian calender all to themselves.

There's something very sombre about November. The very word *November* seems to have a resonance of things ending and dying. Nature has worked its way through the promise of Spring, the high-point of summer, the gathering of Autumn and packed its bags for the deadening feel of Winter. The leaves scattered under our feet are a sad anthem for the decline of another year. It's no coincidence that November is the time of the year when we especially remember our dead.

Because November is a time for remembering. Memory sweeps up the scattered leaves of time and we forage through them to pick and choose the memories that satisfy us or trouble us: the places, the events and especially the people who have shaped and formed us and who drift into our consciousness at this time of the year.

Of course, memory can deceive. Retrospect can camouflage the reality. For memory is a sieve that can refuse to allow some bits of reality to come through. The truth, someone said, is fabled by the daughters of memory and the words with which we sometimes describe the past can disguise the truth.

But no matter how we camouflage the past, it sometimes insists on forcing itself into our consciousness. Walking along a road or driving a car or pottering around the house and suddenly the leaves of yesteryear blow into a heap in front of us and memory takes over.

It's natural to remember and it's part of that nature to remember the dead because they are part of what we are. They have shaped us and formed us in ways it takes a lifetime to explore. We are what we are because of what they have been and memory forces us to pay attention.

As a child I remember the visits to the Church on All Souls Day 'for the souls in purgatory.' We notched the indulgences up as a kind of ransom and we passed each other out, running into and out of the church, to free as many souls as we reasonably could. We visited the graveyard for the same purpose, and were continually reprimanded for the pace of our reluctant piety and the emphasis we placed on the score we were effortlessly keeping.

Now in calmer, more tranquil November days we facilitate the past as we turn over the events of yesteryear in our minds. November is that time of year, a time for remembering those who have gone, searching for a face in the mind's eye, re-telling an almost forgotten story, dredging the memory to keep the focus on times and people fading into the distance. Out thoughts turn inevitably to our own departed loved ones and the discomforting approach of our own deaths. And we do this not just to echo the message that nature sends to us with the coming of Winter. We do it to put a shape on life: to remember, lest we forget.

The poet Philip Larkin dismissed the whole support-system that religion represents as:

That vast moth-eaten musical brockade
Created to pretend we never die.

But the truth is that without it, there is no texture to life, no purpose in death, no support-system to point a direction out of the maze of anxiety and bleakness that attends death, no tradition hallowed by centuries of practice, no vocabulary of remembering.

Part of that remembering is prayer: Masses for the Holy Souls, prayers hallowed with time, recollecting in the presence of God the thoughts that accompany our remembering of the dead. And visiting the cemetery.

There's something about a cemetery in November. It's not just that the fullness of Summer's life has gone ragged or that the graves are easier to tidy. It's something to do with the dampness and the cold and the atmosphere of a cemetery in November. Walking through the graves, reading the headstones, allowing the memories to surface – somehow we feel reassured about who we are and what we believe. Nowhere are we closer to our own roots than walking in our own graveyard. To avoid the experience is to avoid our memories. To forget them is to lose track of ourselves.

So in November we remember the dead. It's a time too of praying for them, of visiting and tidying their graves. For all of us every November, the leaves of time will be swept by memory into the small and great heaps that give birth to our remembering. We remember, lest we forget.

How much do we lose in trying to get what we think we want but don't really need? Parents working so hard that they lose contact with their own children and then in later years regret the false priorities they set themselves. Couples waiting for their children to be reared before they can focus properly on their own relationship and then when the children are gone suddenly realising that there is no relationship to focus on.

How much of what we have do we need?

An investment banker from the United States was at the pier of a coastal Mexican village when a small boat with just one fisherman docked. Inside the boat were several large yellow-fin tuna. The banker complimented the Mexican on the quality of the fish and asked how long it took to catch them.

'Only a little while' replied the Mexican. The banker asked why he didn't stay out longer and catch more fish and the Mexican said he had enough to support his family's immediate needs.

The banker then asked "But what do you do with the rest of your time?"

The Mexican fisherman said 'I sleep late in the morning, fish a little, play with my children, take a siesta with my wife, and stroll into the village each evening where I sip wine and play the guitar with my friends. I have a full and busy life.'

The investment banker scoffed: 'You should spend more time fishing and, with the proceeds, buy a bigger boat. With the proceeds from the bigger boat you could buy several boats. Eventually you could buy a fleet of fishing boats. Instead of selling your catch to a middleman you could sell directly to a processor, eventually opening up your own cannery. You would have to leave this little village, of course, and move to Mexico City, then maybe to Los Angeles and eventually New York if the business continued to thrive.'

The Mexican fisherman asked 'But how long would this take?'

The banker replied 'Maybe 15 to 20 years.'

'But what would I do then?' the fisherman asked

The banker laughed out loud and said 'But don't you see, that's the best part of it. When the time is right you could float your company on the stock market, you could sell your stock to the public and become a very rich man. You could make millions.'

And the fisherman asked him 'And what would I do then?'

The investment banker said 'Well, then you could retire. You could move to a small coastal village, where you could sleep the morning, fish a little, play with your children, take a siesta with your wife, stroll to the village in the evenings where you could sip wine and play your guitar with your friends.'

There are different versions of that story doing the rounds. The above version appeared in *The Tablet* and it's a kind of parable for our time. In an age of incredible prosperity (for some people at least) questions that beg to be asked are: how much of what we have do we really need? Can we distinguish between needs and wants? Can we get off the merry-go-round of work to give ourselves the space and the time to make distinctions between what matters and what is peripheral? Have we got to the stage when we begin to believe that the value of something is the same as the price we pay for it?

How much do we lose in trying to get what we think we want but don't really need? Parents working so hard that they lose contact with their own children and then in later years regret the false priorities they set themselves. An individual postponing something indefinitely until the optimum circumstances prevail and then he or she sees their happiness flowing through their fingers like sea sand. Couples waiting for their children to be reared before they can focus properly on their own relationship and then when the children are gone suddenly realising that there is no relationship to focus on. Workers running themselves into the ground producing things that their families don't really value.

A whole generation sold on a series of wants converted into needs by the advertising industry and ending up with houses full of useless and unused material.

How many video recorders are actually used? How many holidays in the sun were actually worth it? How much of the clutter we have in our house now does anyone use or actually need?

The point is that in a world where everything is moving so quickly and so many decisions are taken on the run, we need to get off the thread-mill and ask ourselves some searching questions on the difference between wants and needs and the price we'll eventually pay for confusing them. To do that we need space and time to unspill the lives we live and to pick through them them in order to establish priorities.

Getting someone to have a word with someone was part of the way politics worked in Ireland. It was so engrained in Irish life that even when people were entitled to something, like the old age pension, they felt that they had to go through the routine of asking a politician to 'intervene' for them – even though no intervention was necessary.

Putting a word in

JOHN Healy, the late and distinguished political commentator, never quite understood what made Vincent Browne tick. Political patronage, for example, was part of Healy's world. If your party was in power then you got the benefit of whatever was going. Pulling a stroke for your own was part of the political system.

Browne and his proteges railed against what they perceived to be the abuse of a political system, where *who* you knew was more important than *what* you knew. Where resources were allocated not just in terms of need but political favour. Even though the words are now cliched, what they sought was openness, transparency and accountability, the goddess OTA, as reviled in later years by Charlie McCreevy.

In fairness to Browne, from the early days, he asked the embarrassing questions. Like, asking Charlie Haughey, the sixty thousand dollar question that, despite the tribunals, is still being asked: Charlie, where did you get all your money if you spent all your life in politics?

In later years what 'Haughey', the documentary series on RTÉ television unveiled is the doctrine of political patronage being pressed to its extremes. To such an extent that it has corrupted not just individual politicians, as clearly it has, but the political system itself.

Getting someone to have a word with someone was part of the way politics worked in Ireland. It was so engrained in Irish life that even when people were entitled to something, like the old age pension, they felt that they had to go through the routine of asking a politician to 'intervene' for them – even though no intervention was necessary.

Getting someone to have a word with someone was part of the way everything worked in Ireland. Getting someone 'higher up' to intervene was part of the ethos of the past, part of the disempowerment of people. Getting a job as a teacher involved putting a word in with the priest-manager of the day. Getting a job in a bank meant getting someone with a hefty account to make representations for you. And so on.

Now, of course, it seems curiously old-fashioned, embarrassing, almost malevolent and certainly out of sync with a new and more confident Ireland. But it was part of the ethos of the day. Even to the extent that Vincent Browne himself some years ago found himself having a word with the then Taoiseach of the day, Garret FitzGerald. It later emerged that when *The Sunday Tribune* was in straitened financial circumstances, Browne got in touch with Dr Fitzgerald in order that a meeting might be organised with the revenue commissioners to discuss the situation. The meeting took place, though without the difficulty being resolved.

Nothing untoward happened and neither Browne nor Fitzgerald were in any way guilty of any wrongdoing but what's interesting about the intervention was that Browne was using his position to make contact with a Taoiseach. Not everyone could phone the Taoiseach of the day and put a suggestion to him. In other words, advantage was taken due to position.

The Moriarity tribunal has long focussed on a key question: did Charlie Haughey do any favours for the ten million plus he was given by rich business people while he was Taoiseach? More particularly, why did Ben Dunne give Haughey over two million in the late 1980s?

Dunne and others had access to Haughey because they had money and Haughey felt he needed extra money to keep himself in the lifestyle to which he had become accustomed. So, to accept the more malign view, they used that leverage to get Haughey to do whatever it is they wanted him to do. Or possibly, the benign view, they were so taken with Charlie's personality and his career that they couldn't stop themselves filling out cheques for him.

I'm not in any sense equating the above questions with Browne's intervention with FitzGerald. To say the least, there is a significant qualitative difference between the two. But they have this in common: both used positions to make contact with the Taoiseach of the day. Both operated out of the widely accepted Irish political belief that you get things done by getting to the people in power.

The difficulty is that such a system is open to abuse. And as we watched the Haughey saga unfolding before our eyes we saw how what seemed innocent and practical – 'putting a word in with someone' – can lead to the corruption not just of individuals but of the political life of the country.

There may be widespread unease about how tortuously slow and how incredibly expensive the tribunals are, but what they are in effect doing is peeling back the veneers we have painted to camouflage the less than honourable sleight-of-hand that is at the heart of the body politic in Ireland. At ten times the price, the tribunals are coming cheap. Because what they are reminding us about is not just who was corrupt and who was caught but where the corruption stems from: a way of operating at a political level that allows less than honourable people to act corruptly.

Peeling back those veneers is a painful business. But anyone looking at the Haughey saga could have no doubt about the need for all of us to face the corrupt logic of our culture of 'putting a word in'.

/

We don't notice it, those of us who are on the right side of the track. In fact from the higher ground of economic well-being, we can even convince ourselves that poverty doesn't really exist anymore and if it does it's in tiny pockets or it's their own fault!

The road to God knows where

JOHN Updike, the celebrated American novelist, wrote *Toward the End of Time* in 1997. The novel is set near Boston in the year 2020. A recent war between the United States and China has devastated large tracts of the United States and millions of people have been wiped out. There is social chaos in what's left of America and the remaining population is divided into two groups: the haves who continue to live out their extravagant lifestyles in enclosed compounds while paying protection money to mafia-type gangsters; and the rest of the population who skirt the edges of the defensive compounds of the rich and scavenge to survive. Updike paints a bleak picture of a divided society skirting the edges of survival.

Reading *Toward the End of Time* recently, it struck me that Updike's bizarre scenario had more than a grain of truth in it. I don't know the American scene so I can't really vouch for the defensive mentality that social chaos can bring in its wake. But if the window into American life that television presents to us is anything to go by, American society is already under siege. The line of bolts and locks on the inside of apartment doors is something of an emblem of American life.

But Updike's novel applies nearer home too. Ireland won't have any war with China but a great social division is opening up in Irish life and one day we will surely pay for it. On the one hand we are a spectacularly successful country with phenomenal economic growth this decade. In eight years the numbers employed have grown by almost a third of a million. The national budget is in substantial surplus. Wealth has grown dramatically. On the other hand housing waiting lists have grown spectacularly (doubling in a few years). Rural Ireland is in steep decline. Poverty and deprivation have remained constant. Exclusion has grown. And the gap between rich and poor continues to widen and widen.

We don't notice it, of course, those of us who are on the right side of the track. In fact from the higher ground of economic well-being, we can even convince ourselves that poverty doesn't really exist anymore and if it does it's in tiny pockets or it's their own fault! In other words, we are now part of what the celebrated economist Kenneth Galbraith once called 'the culture of contentment'. What he meant was that with an increased overall prosperity in society a majority of people reach a level where they buy into retaining the status quo. Those who never had it so good tend to forget about those on the wrong side of the track.

A significant and worrying shift is now taking place in Irish society. A huge gap is opening up between those who have a real stake in Irish life (in terms of work, property, political clout, etc) and those who are becoming an under-class. I make no apology for using that word *under-class* because we can no longer delude ourselves with the sentimental notion that Ireland is a classless society. It isn't and I doubt very much if it ever was.

The reality of Irish life is not that a penny is looking down on a halfpenny (as used to be the case) but that a euro is looking down on a cent. And that reality is not just evident in large cities but even in rural towns. You see it in the social scene (golf versus bingo), in educational mobility (one of those nicer out-of-town schools instead of the rougher set in town), even in accent. And anyone who suggests that we're a classless society has only to look at the social patterns of upper-class and middle-class towns. There are middle-class kids who have never stood and will never ever stand in a working-class home.

The hope was that the great tide of prosperity would lift all boats. But, as Fr Sean Healy of CORI often said, a rising tide is no good to those with no boats! Instead the rich have become progressively richer and the poor progressively poorer. The gap is widening and a ravaged underclass is gradually forming. That underclass will inevitably become more excluded, more desperate, more violent, more criminal and less inclined to accept the social limits that their betters will try to impose on them. And we already know the damage that even a handful of desperate people can do.

There are fancy words we use like *social cohesion* to describe a society that in the main respected common rules and common boundaries. There is a concept we call *inclusion* to describe a shared responsibility for one another. And the more we talk in such terms the more we realise that someday our society is going to pay a terrible price for the widening gap between rich and poor. For years Mr. McCreevy's budgets widened the gap between rich and poor and kept us firmly on the road to only God knows where. Can Mr Cowen (or Mr Rabbitte) undo the damage?

The old curmudgeons were cut from a different cloth. Like Ford cars,
they all came in black, and so the impression was given that they were
all the same. Far from it. Difference and eccentricity were somehow
exacerbated by the impression of sameness. Of course, clerical life
provided a conducive environment for eccentricity to prosper.
Clerical eccentricity is one of the few fruits of celibacy.

The grace of eccentricity

*O*dd is an odd word. We tend to use it to describe other people. But
it's a trifle disconcerting to hear it used about oneself. Priests, the
woman said in a voice loud enough to attract attention, are a rather *odd*
lot. And she stressed the word *odd*. Clearly *odd* wasn't meant in its
literal sense, the opposite of *even*. What she meant was *abnormal* or,
more kindly, *eccentric*. I have problems with the word *abnormal* but I
can take *eccentric* because in a way I see it as a grace, God's way of
ensuring that the human race is embellished with more variety that
even Mr Heinz contemplated.

Priests may well be eccentric but, if anything, I think we're less
eccentric than we were. Which is a great pity. The younger generation
of clerics seems to be cut from a more predictable cloth. There are
fewer characters than heretofore and many of them, to my mind, too
serious and, even worse, too pious by half.

You wouldn't like to be caught on a desert island with a bunch of
them. It would be prayer for breakfast, dinner and tea. God would
never get a day off.

The old curmudgeons were cut from a different cloth. Like Ford
cars, they all came in black, and so the impression was given that they
were all the same. Far from it. Difference and eccentricity were

159

somehow exacerbated by the impression of sameness. Of course, clerical life provided a conducive environment for eccentricity to prosper. Apart from a few fussy housekeepers, there was no one to temper excesses of oddness. The most eccentric behaviour can eventually appear completely natural if there is no one to call a halt. Clerical eccentricity is one of the few fruits of celibacy.

The late John F.X. Harriott, who wrote his inimitable *Periscope* column in *The Tablet* for many years once described an elderly PP in the north of England whose presbytery lay alongside a public park frequented by courting couples. Every twilight he kept vigil by his window and at the least sight or sound – the rustle of a branch, a low whisper or a hint of laughter on the breeze – he blew a referee's whistle. Enough there to keep a gaggle of psychotherapists happy for the winter.

Or the time when Confessions at Christmas meant overtime in the confessional. A character who had spent hours in the box disposing of mortal sins and venial sins with no sign of the queue ending eventually lost his patience, flung open the door of the confessional and announced 'From now on I'm only hearing mortal sins.' The queue evaporated in seconds.

One priest whom I knew only vaguely had devised his own system of writing music and even though he hadn't a note in his head was able to compose new and frighteningly original material. He once played an original composition for me and asked me what I thought of it. It was, to my unpractised ear, the musical equivalent of a suit of clothes sewn by a blind tailor. But he could hardly conceal his delight in the revolutionary breakthrough he had accomplished even though no one was impressed but himself. He also used to bring a bicycle with him for a walk because he was harrassed by people stopping their cars offering him a lift.

Part of the difficulty, of course, is that as the years go on, we need others to recognise eccentricity. Some people, for instance, regard a healthy allergy to parties as an indication of impending oddness. For my own part I have a recurring nightmare that I will beset in my old age by a condition which might render me incapable of communicating with those around me. The apex of this nightmare is being taken to an endless number of mindless celebrations by a social freak who's idea of heaven is a cross between a party and a sing-song. And being reassured, that it's for your own good, my dear.

It's all of course a question of balance. Eccentrics, like a drunk weaving along the parapet of a bridge, have an unerring instinct for startling or amusing behaviour whilst drawing short of anything that might just encourage someone to send for the men in white coats. There is a benign predictability to their behaviour that eventually reassures. While the rest of us describe things in black or white or occasionally grey, they come out all psychedelic. They were lateral thinkers before anyone knew what the words meant. And, God bless them, they bring an air of necessary unreality to the predictable and boring lives most of us tend to live.

Eccentricity, as John Harriott wrote, is a special kind of grace.

People often comment now on the decline of community in Ireland. It's said that people are becoming more private and individualistic. But how much of it I wonder has to do with people simply creating a private space for themselves? How much has it to do with people resisting any public intrusion into their lives? Could it be no more than a natural reaction to the pervasive curiosity and intrusiveness that's almost endemic in Irish society?

Neurotic curiosity

DURING the 80s, when emigration to the United States was at its peak, I remember having a conversation with a group of young Irishmen and women in New York. The general view was that they wanted to stash away as much money as they could, as quickly as they could, and then return to Ireland, build a house, get married and raise a family. But a few had a different strategy. Their plan was to get as far away from Ireland as they could and to stay as far away as they could, for as long as they could. For them emigrating wasn't so much an economic necessity as an opportunity to fill their lungs with the fresh air of freedom.

While those who wanted to return home regretted the vast anonymity of New York, others saw it as a relief from the oppressive and insular society they had let behind. I remember at the time wondering whether Ireland was really that bad. And I remember deciding, on reflection, that yes, we were that bad. Sometimes the problem is that oppressiveness - or lack of privacy or intrusiveness or sheer plain nosiness or whatever words you want to put on it – is so much part of our culture that often we don't see it at all. Sometimes we imagine that the obsessive even pathological curiosity Irish people are endowed with is as natural as butter. And sometimes it's only when we get away from it that we realise how neurotic it often is.

A few examples. Some time ago a priest died in a rural parish. He had, it seems, spent what parishioners regarded as an inordinate sum of money renovating the house. He resented this assessment and decided to get his own back by refusing to show parishioners round the house after the renovation was completed. When someone called to the parochial house his practice was to usher them into a small office adjacent to the door. There was no entry into the inner chamber and the more entry was denied the more inquisitive people became and the more exaggerated the stories were.

Then the priest died suddenly after a short illness. When word spread that he was laid out in the house, hordes of people descended on the property not in truth to pray for the poor man but to get a look at the house. People even came from neighbouring parishes. People who hardly knew where the parochial house was came to pay their respects and often got short taken (as we say) as a way of gaining admittance to what was, by all accounts, a quite exotic bathroom.

Another example. A couple moved into an area. They used separate names, as is often now the practice. And locals began to wonder whether in fact they were married or not. A well known religious neurotic who was so far off the wall as to be at the end of the back garden set himself the task of unmasking this mystery in the interests of maintaining the moral fibre or the religious ethos of the area or whatever words justified this curiosity. Enquiries were made as to where the newcomers were from, what they did for a living, what papers they read, even what groceries they happened to buy in a local shop. Eventually our neurotic friend took it on himself to ask them directly: 'People were wondering . . . ' Murder has been committed for less.

People often comment now on the decline of community in Ireland. It's said that people are becoming more private and individualistic; that visiting or rambling is becoming a thing of the past; that television has ruined conversation and story-telling; that houses are becoming impenetrable fortresses after 6 pm in the evening.

But how much of it I wonder has to do with people simply creating a private space for themselves? How much has it to do with people resisting any public intrusion into their lives? Could it be no more than a natural reaction to the pervasive curiosity and intrusiveness that's almost endemic in Irish society?

Someone said to me recently that the decline in Station Masses is an indication of the decline in community in rural Ireland. And that may well be true. At a time when houses were never better many people simply just don't want to know about Station Masses. But could it be that it's simply a way of avoiding what some people regard as an unacceptable intrusion.

I remember once hearing confession at a Station Mass in a bedroom and while the penitent was saying her Act of Contrition she was examining what was under the bed while I could see the whole performance in the mirror of the wardrobe! There she was, as the old saying goes, examining more than her conscience. Or when people turn away priests from the door (as now happens quite often in town parishes) is it because they're disinterested in religion or because they resent church intrusion into their lives?

Could it be that some can't see our neurotic inquisitiveness because it's so much part of the air that we breathe but that some people do and they're opting out, thank you very much. And, you know, it's hard to blame them.

As attendance at the ceremonies of Holy Week continues to decline
and as liturgists, with unerring instinct, continue to lose the plot, the
silver lining to these particular clouds is a growing respect for the
creative and the imaginative in Christian ritual.
Ritual needs to spread its wings and soar into the distance

Creative ritual

SO how did you get over the Easter? Not a question we're often
asked, unlike its Christmas equivalent. But a fair question
nonetheless. Or could I put it another way: had you an Easter to get
over? There was the holiday weekend. There were the great sporting
events. Family members came home. Pubs did a roaring trade. Shops
were busy. But what about Easter? Not Easter, the bank holiday
weekend but Easter, the great religious feast of the year. Or did its
religious significance really impinge on our consciousness?

Yes, I know there were great crowds at the Masses on Easter
Sunday. Visitors were home and mothers bid the reluctant from bed to
pew as mothers are wont to do. But Easter Sunday is a bit like the
turkey sandwiches a few days after Christmas. You get the flavour but
you miss the essence. You think you were there but you've somehow
missed the experience.

The writer Denis Tuohy, in a contribution to *The Tablet*, explained
that periodically he takes a reflective break in a retreat-house. During a
break this Lent, he was leaving the house for a ruminative stroll when
he struck up a conversation with a man of the roads who had called to
the retreat house. He was a big, white-bearded Scotsman who told him
that he loved the run-up to Easter. 'Let me tell you why' he confided.

'It's because it reminds me that he walked this earth, this same earth we walk upon.

Does Easter *excite* you? Probably not, if the truth be told. Part of the difficulty is that Holy Week, most of the time and for most people, is either ignored in its entirety or regarded as something to be got through, a penance to be endured. *Excitement* isn't the first word that comes to mind. Even for those of us charged with the responsibility of leading people in celebrating what is the greatest feast of the year, excitement seemed to be in short supply. Yes, I know priests can get excited about a variety of personal or even official tasks. But, in practice, Holy Week is often a marathon that we struggle through rather than an exciting opportunity to celebrate the great events that are at the heart of our faith.

So what can we do to rediscover the excitement of Holy Week? Part of the answer might be to take some of it outside the church. Over the years thousands of people have attended the annual Passion Play in the grounds of Ballintubber Abbey, a natural amphitheatre for staging a dramatic event. And what better way to remember and celebrate the passion and death of Jesus than by reliving in dramatic form the great events of Holy Week? And what an enriching and satisfying experience it is in comparison to a simple reading of the text.

Obviously, the Ballintubber production would be beyond most parishes but surely there is a case to be made for a number of parishes to cancel their individual Good Friday ceremonies and combine their resources in presenting a Passion Play in a convenient place. Yes, I know that there are a thousand arguments against it, but just imagine the *excitement* it would generate!

What I think we need for a renewed focus on Holy Week is a creative, imaginative and, above all, a dramatic approach to the Holy Week Ceremonies. We need to get out of the confining space of our minds and our churches. This was brought home to me very forcibly one year when the faith-community of Kilglass in County Sligo, of which I was a part, gathered for a dawn Mass on Easter Sunday morning. Before 6.00 a.m. the people gathered. The church was in darkness, lit with just a few candles. As Mass progressed, the dawn broke and the light gradually increased until it streamed through the windows, breaking away the darkness of the night. I found it an extremely moving experience. But why in the church? Why not on Enniscrone beach where the symbolism of the rising sun would seep into our souls? You can see why John O'Donohue takes to the Burren country.

Part of the problem is that we don't give ourselves permission to be creative in ritual. We are so stuck in routine and in rubric that we almost instinctively avoid what might raise the siege that a numbing repetition and predictability bring to matters liturgical.

An Anglican priest once became very upset over the removal of an asterisk from the official Prayer Book version of the *Nunc Dimittis*. The asterisk came at a very awkward place: "For mine eyes have seen * thy salvation." A director of music had removed the asterisk to facilitate the musical flow of the phrase. The priest objected. 'Once you remove one asterisk, it's all up for grabs.'

In a way he was right. Because once the printed page or the liturgist's gloss are not absolute then the door to creativity can be prised open. Of course, we give liturgists too much room. In matters liturgical, as we know, there are three divisions. There's 'the premiership', where experts debate about the progress of translations through the incomprehensible maze that we know and love as the ICEL. (The official international translation committee of the Roman Catholic Church.) This is 'O Antiphons' country. But its often esoteric concerns rarely connect with life or experience.

Then there's the 'first division', the routine of specialised courses where local experts are wheeled in at irregular intervals to reproduce in some confused way what the experts would tell us if they were here. And finally there's a 'second division', to which the rest of us have been relegated, where liturgy has to happen as distinct from being talked about, where imagination and variety are the spice of liturgical life and where sometimes to make things work or 'connect' you have to bend and sometimes ignore the rules.

As attendance at the ceremonies of Holy Week continues to decline and as liturgists, with unerring instinct, continue to lose the plot, the silver lining to these particular clouds is a growing respect for the creative and the imaginative in Christian ritual. Just as the preaching of the gospel is inhibited by the predictable pattern of pulpit and parson and will need to escape from its musty surroundings to stand its ground in a different world, so too ritual needs to spread its wings and soar into the distance.

167

As I walk around the shops at Christmas-time, a sound or a sight or a smell suddenly re-awakens something within me. It could be an echo of a Christmas carol or a child's face in the crowd or an old person shuffling along. And suddenly a memory comes flooding back. A seasonal wistfulness follows as I remember the faces and places of the Christmases of the past.

Ghosts of Christmas past

IT'S always the same on Christmas night. No matter where I am or who I'm with. Invariably the same image pushes it's way to the very front of my mind. I'm a child again and I'm kneeling in the kitchen at home in Ballycastle as we say the Rosary on Christmas night. I'm watching the rest of the family, eight in all, through the rails of a kitchen chair. Waiting for the rosary to be over. Waiting to get to bed so that I won't keep Santa Claus waiting. And then as the litany ends and my father blesses himself he says, 'Go mbeirimid beo ar an am seo arís.' And even though I'm a child, even though the Irish is a bit strange to me, I know what it means - a prayer that we may be all alive and well for the next Christmas.

That memory is as vivid as yesterday and I know that as long as I live that memory of a Christmas past will remain with me. Probably because, for the first time in my young life, I suddenly realised that the little securities that I had built around my childhood weren't necessarily permanent. Santa Claus always turned up on Christmas night; the carcass of the plucked turkey was always singed over a plate of lighted methylated spirits in a Christmas Eve ritual; the giblets were always ready in the pot; the three Masses on Christmas morning would always seem interminably long as we waited to get home to the toys; but my father's words had placed a question-mark at the heart of Christmas and at the heart of life. Some Christmas would come and we wouldn't all be there.

It's called growing up. Suddenly we realise that there are darker, less benign realities in life and that someday some of them are going to knock on our door. Someday we would say the Rosary and there would be more decades than family to lead them. Someday the prevailing winds would be harsher than I had as yet imagined.

I remember going to bed and waiting for Santa Claus to come. My older brothers would shout up the stairs to say that Santa Claus had been sighted at the top of the town but that if we weren't asleep he might pass the house. And we tried to close our eyes and will ourselves to sleep.

Then in the morning there was the excitement of getting the toys and the fruit and the bag of sweets. Even though Santa Claus had come from the North Pole what he brought always bore an uncanny resemblance to what we had seen the day before in Polke's shop. And then the trek to the chapel in the dark as people gathered.

As every Christmas approaches my thoughts go back to the kitchen in Ballycastle and my father praying for all of us to make it to another Christmas.

For all the oppressive camouflage of sound and sight, Christmas has a funny way of creating an empty space around us. Despite the hype, Christmas has a way of stripping our lives down to the essentials. In the midst of Christmas cheer, a small thin voice insists on posing a series of difficult questions. And we find ourselves putting our lives under a microscope. Wondering. And thanking. And hoping. And cherishing – while we still have the chance.

It's the equivalent of shuffling our way through a dense forest and then suddenly we find ourselves in a calm, silent clearance. And we get a calmer and more reflective view of where we are. Suddenly we have an opportunity to put things in perspective. It's as if, in some peculiar way, we have been brought into our own presence.

As I walk around the shops at Christmas-time, a sound or a sight or a smell suddenly re-awakens something within me. It could be an echo of a Christmas carol or a child's face in the crowd or an old person shuffling along. And suddenly a memory comes flooding back. A seasonal wistfulness follows as I remember the faces and places of the Christmases of the past. Then more reflectively I begin to place the hopes and the dreams in the context of where it's at. And I can feel the edge of regret and failure. Tread softly, someone said, for you tread on my dreams.

And Christmas is a funny time. As in that kitchen of my childhood, looking out through the cream-coloured rails of the chair, Christmas makes me feel at once elated and depressed, happy and sad. Something within me wants to open the great tabernacle of memories and hug them to bits. Something else wants us to close that tabernacle tight, to hold memory at a distance.

I see in the distance a couple embracing. I see people with children and without children. I watch an old man struggling to get across a street. I look at the intensity in the eyes of a child in a crowded shop and something flutters within me. A tears wells up or a smile breaks out. Something reminds me of how happy or unhappy I am, how fractured and how fragile are the bits and pieces of yesteryear that come to me out of the shadows.

Nuala O'Faoláin walked alone on the Burren on Christmas day, a study in isolation. Paul Durcan writes about watching a phone on St Stephen's Day that never rings. Few of us would want to confront our demons so harshly. But at Christmas time, the memories slip through the sieve of life and the demons gather, demanding a space, searching for an audience. Christmas is that kind of time. It's the great tabernacle of memories. Memories, good and bad but never indifferent. Memories that bring a warmth and a happiness with them and memories too that leave us desolate and cold. Hopes remembered, dreams relived, that middle ground between the possible and the actual re-tilled over and over until we begin to see the fruits of our lives scattered around our feet.

This Christmas let the water under your feet settle into a little puddle so that you can see a bit of yourself in it. Let the bustle fade into a silence. Find a clear space where you can hear what life is saying to you. Sit somewhere and look out at the world as it rages and races past. Find a quiet corner and let the ghosts of Christmases past come to the surface. Christmas is another clearance and it's always in the clearances that we find out what really matters. Like the little boy looking through the rails of that kitchen chair so many years ago.

*Drunkenness in Irish society isn't funny. But give a few people
a few jars and suddenly, regardless of the circumstances, our
extraordinary naivety towards and tolerance for drinking
and drunkenness click in and we find ourselves mouthing
a series of euphemisms that mask the grim reality behind
our boozing culture*

Drunk drivers

I was once called to the scene of an accident in the early hours of the morning. A number of cars - coming from a party and going in the same direction - had piled up and a few people were injured, none seriously. When I arrived a few young men in their twenties were trapped inside a car and members of the fire service were hacking through the tangled metal of the remains of a car, trying to release them.

A doctor stood by waiting to render medical assistance. At this stage it wasn't clear how significant the injuries were. Or indeed if someone had been killed. At one point, when the din of the cutting equipment subsided, a voice from the depths of the confusion rang out with an inebriated version of *The Fields of Athenry*. The crowd gathered around the wreckage broke into relieved laughter whereupon the doctor turned angrily on them and said, 'This isn't funny. There's nothing funny about this'.

The man had a point. Drunkenness in Irish society isn't funny. It wasn't funny then and it's less funny now. And standing in the dark beside the tangled remains of a few cars wondering what the extent of the injuries will be when the fire brigade has finished cutting open the side of a car is, for most people, particularly unfunny.

But give a few people a few jars and suddenly, regardless of the circumstances, our extraordinary naivety towards and tolerance for drinking and drunkenness click in and we find ourselves mouthing a series of euphemisms that mask the grim reality behind our boozing culture.

When the dust settles, there's nothing funny about people who drink to excess. For the simple reason that they bring extraordinary unhappiness into the lives of those around them. George Best, one of the great drinkers of the twentieth century and a man who helped millions to laugh indulgently at his life of excess, called a tabloid newspaper to his death-bed to take a photograph so that millions could see for themselves the consequences of his boozy lifestyle. It wasn't a jolly picture.

But, we say, that was George. Good old George. No salutary lesson there because George was different, larger-than-life. A flawed genius. But it's not just about George. It's about all the ordinary geniuses who adamantly turn a blind eye to the consequences of our drinking culture. It's about all who see bank holidays or great sporting days as an occasion to get drunk, to lose control of their faculties, to wander around aimlessly because the pubs had closed or the money was gone until someone pointed them in the direction of home. And when they arrive home they terrorise their own children, beat their wives (or husbands) and wake up the next day suitably chastened by the unhappiness they have brought to their nearest and dearest, the money they have wasted, the idiots they have made of themselves.

Sometimes I really wish there was no St Patrick's Day. Or Mayo getting to the All Ireland final. And what a blessed relief it will be to so many families if the Republic of Ireland don't make it to Europe next summer.

Imagine the sheer mountain of pain and upset and collateral damage, psychological and otherwise, drunks inflict on those around them under the guise of drowning the shamrock or cheering on their heroes. Imagine the dividend in family contentment of Steve Staunton's failure to lead his men to Europe.

Imagine the money families would have for the things that really matter. Imagine not having to listen to, still less applaud, some idiot bragging about his ability to consume huge quantities of drink.

172

Imagine not having to listen to idiots the morning after trying to convince themselves that they had a great night even though they can't remember most of it.

Who would want to be a Garda on duty on a busy bank holiday weekend? Dealing with all that mayhem and nonsense. Or a nurse or doctor in *Accident and Emergency*. Or a priest standing in the middle of a kitchen trying to help ease a way for families out of the uproar and conflict generated by one family member's drinking, knowing that this distressing scene is being replicated in every parish in Ireland. And will be replicated in this family every time there's an excuse for a booze-up.

What can we possibly do anymore about our binge-drinking culture? No matter how graphic the television pictures. No matter how many icons like George Best are pictured on their death-beds on the front page of the largest-selling tabloid newspaper. No matter how many statistics are crunched for our edification. No matter who says what to whom.

The message just doesn't get through. Drink is the great killer in Ireland today. Drink is the greatest destroyer of family life. Drink is the most abused drug in our society. Drink is the greatest cause of unhappiness in homes. Drink costs the country a fortune in workdays lost and so on.

Yet everything in our culture contrives to deny its devastating consequences.

So let's not indulge our drunks anymore. Let's refuse to listen to the next drunken bore who wants us to be impressed by the dimensions of his blather. Let's refuse to laugh at all the boozy jokes about the drunken Irish, God love them and their talent for enjoying themselves.

The doctor on the side of the road was right. There's nothing funny about drink. And only those who don't have to pick up the pieces, literally or metaphorically, can afford to laugh at drink anymore.

The antidote to being harrassed and hassled is the simple, straightforward advice about making a little space, creating a still centre so that we call find our bearings in the noisy, moving world around us. The question is: Where is 'the lonely place' where we can be by ourselves that helps to give us a perspective on things so that we can distinguish what's important from what, relatively speaking, isn't important at all?

Finding a lonely place

THERE are some very sharp turnings in life. Most of us most of the time settle into a pattern of living and we imagine that it will go on forever. It doesn't, of course, because life is full of turnings - sudden death, serious illness, broken relationships. A phone call, a knock on the door, a tap on the shoulder and from that point on nothing is ever the same. We never know, as the cliche has it, what's around the next corner.

The trick is not to become lulled into accepting the present as a predictable pattern. The trick is to see the present moment as the good times that in future years we'll look back on with fond memories.

Easier said than done. Especially today when everyone is so busy. Everyone caught on a merry-go-round of activity. So few creating any kind of space to find an opportunity 'to smell the roses.' Where has all the time gone, Michel Quoist, asked in his famous book , *Prayers for Life*, nearly forty years ago?

It's a more pertinent question now. I remember lapping hay in the summers of my childhood. We shook out the hay. We raked it into wind-rows. We lapped it. Then if a mist swept in from Shrahloggagh we shook it out again and we made it into breast-cocks. Then we shook it out again . . . Recently I watched huge tractors descending on a ten-acre meadow and two hours later the whole crop was in a sileage pit in the corner of the field.

The same applies to all the work we do, the transport we enjoy, the facilities we have at in our homes. We never had so many time-saving devices and yet we never had so little time. Where is the time going? And how can we deal with the stress that comes from never having enough of it to do the things we want to do?

Open practically any newspaper or magazine now and you'll find something about stress or pressure or tension. And invariably the antidote to it is the same advice Jesus gave his apostles two thousand years ago: 'Go away to some lonely place all by yourselves and rest for a while.'

The antidote to being harrassed and hassled is the simple, straightforward advice about making a little space, creating a still centre so that we call find our bearings in the noisy, moving world around us. The question is: Where is 'the lonely place' where we can be by ourselves that helps to give us a perspective on things so that we can distinguish what's important from what, relatively speaking, isn't important at all? Where is the still centre that helps us to keep our priorities right?

Everyone needs this 'lonely place'. Everyone needs an experience of stillness, silence, solitude. Everyone needs to let life sit with them so that the cares and concerns of life can be placed in a healthy context. Some people visit a quiet church and sit before the tabernacle and let the cares and worries of life fall around them. Just sitting there. Maybe at first getting into the mood of stillness by listening to the beat of your own heart, or to your breathing. And letting the thoughts come. Creating a space. And giving it time.

Others like to go for a long walk along a beach and use the rhythm of their walking to calm the demons within them so that they can get outside themselves in order to see reality with a clarity and a vision that gives them a different perspective on life.

Others go away for a whole day, bring a packed lunch, walk a bit, sit by a stream, read a book that stimulates a quiet, still reflection on the lives they lead, the people they love, the work they do, the time they spend on the priorities in their lives. Away from the children and spouse and home. Away by themselves. Mammy's day for herself, as I heard children describe it once.

That's one part of the message. The other is that you come back out of silence, stillness, solitude into the mainstream of life again. And the real trick is in balancing the two. We need to break off from the hustle and bustle of our busy lives and find a lonely place. And we need to get back too into the bustle of life, accepting our responsibilities and commitments. Because out of silence and solitude, out of reflection and prayer, out of that lonely place will come a renewed commitment to the lives and responsibilities that God has given to each one of us.

There is, I believe, a road to that lonely place that, like the apostles, God wants each one of us to take. But there is a road too out of that lonely place that leads us back into the activity and the movement of the life God has given us and the commitments and responsibilities that flow from it.

Mother Teresa made it a rule for her nuns, that even in the busiest of places, the windows of their chapels are left open to let the noise in, to help them make the connection between prayer and life, between the still centre we all need and the bustle of life that is part of what we are.

Going into silence and solitude is not about denying the importance of much of the frenetic activity of our lives. Because that's life today. Rather it's about giving ourselves a clearer view of the things that really matter.

An effort is being made to reform the reform of the liturgy that took place in the years after the Second Vatican Council. And part of the intention of restoring the old is a rejection of the new. The modern – language, music, presentation – is too thin, we're told, to carry the transcendent and we have to go back to the old to recapture the splendour, solemnity and dignity of the Mass.

Longing for Latin

There are suggestions emanating from Rome that the new liturgy, which is perceived to lack the reverence and solemnity of the old rites, needs to be revamped. For the first time in twenty years a Tridentine Mass (the old pre-Vatican Two Latin Mass) was recently celebrated in the crypt at St Peter's Basilica in Rome. Some time back the first public old-rite Confirmations in Britain for over thirty years were celebrated in St Bede's Catholic Church in London. And a few years ago Pope Benedict XVI when he was Cardinal Ratzinger wrote a preface to a book which argues that altars should be changed back again and priests should say Mass with their backs to the people!

So what's happening? Clearly an effort is being made to reform the reform of the liturgy that took place in the years after the Second Vatican Council. And part of the intention of restoring the old is a rejection of the new. The modern – language, music, presentation – is too thin, we're told, to carry the transcendent and we have to go back to the old to recapture the splendour, solemnity and dignity of the Mass.

I'm far from convinced, I have to say. For a number of reasons. One is that memory can play a lot of tricks on us. When experience is pushed through the sieve of memory, we often remember the best of it, like the great summers of yesteryear.

A few years ago I attended a Latin Mass in Knock. Some Latin Mass society had organised it and it had all the trimmings that I remembered from the old High Mass: the priest had his back to the people; everything was in Latin except the sermon; incense was widely used; the Creed and other parts of the Mass were sung in the form of Gregorian Chant; there was no Sign of Peace; and there were no altar girls. I came away from it relieved and grateful that we had left it behind us.

What struck me about it was how tepid the whole experience was and how detached the congregation was from what was happening. People said the rosary or whatever prayers they wanted to say and the priest might as well have been in Limerick. There was no sense at all of participation or connection. There was no engagement. Everything seemed to conspire to keep the congregation at a distance: the Latin language, the lack of understanding of the readings, the unfamiliar Gregorian chant; the priest just getting on with what seemed a private ceremony.

What was especially devastating about the experience was that this was the honours version of the Latin Mass. There was an organist, a choir, a priest with a *Latin blas*, all involved were meticulously prepared and so forth. This wasn't the everyday version of the Latin Mass in the average country parish where naturally enough the standards weren't quite so high. And yet it seemed pallid and distant in comparison to the new rite.   Indeed the only sense of mystery came from the fact that very few if any could understand what was going on. I'm not too sure that really qualifies as mystery.

The other point that struck me was that for the old Latin Mass to work you had to have a certain education, a certain level of appreciation. In that sense there was a certain elitism associated with it. Just as there often is now with Latin Mass enthusiasts who see themselves as a bit above your average Catholic who really doesn't know as much as they do. They often regard themselves as 'real Catholics' as distinct from other less enlightened versions.

We tend to forget how inadequate as liturgy the old Mass often was in the average parish church where a small choir had to struggle with the intricacies of Gregorian Chant, where the people didn't understand the readings, where the priest struggled through the Latin, where the server stumbled through the few responses and where people attended rather than participated. When Cardinals in Rome muse nostalgically on the solemnity and reverence of the old liturgy what they have in mind is showpiece liturgies in St Peter's Basilica not your average parish church.

One criticism of the new Mass is that priests rush through it without giving it the attention and the time it deserves. I get letters regularly from a harrassed worshipper who is regularly scandalised by the indecent haste with which her PP gets through the Mass. A member of the *Fast Mass Appreciation Society*, he seems to take a certain pride in having them 'in and out' in fifteen minutes flat! She pines for the ease and solemnity and sense of wonder that the Latin Mass invoked.

But the problem is not with the new Mass but with the Very Reverend Michael Schumachers. We all have memories of the Latin Mass when Canon Stirling Moss went through a Mass that was twice as long in as little as twelve and a half minutes . . . and all in a language no one understood. There was more reverence and solemnity at Brand's Hatch.

Reverence, an air of solemnity, a sense of wonder have to do with attitude, approach, faith rather than a particular style of Mass. Longing for the old Latin Mass is about nostalgia, not religion. The truth is that if we re-introduced the Latin Mass our congregations would probably disappear altogether.

The overwhelming feeling of relief that the republican movement has at long last recognised the futility of what they called 'armed conflict' has to be balanced by a reasonable question about the wisdom of trusting their word. The Sunday before the final act of decommissioning Sinn Féin organised a united Ireland rally .

A beginning, not an ending

AT long last, after all the huffing and puffing, the IRA has conceded that the SDLP were right after all. Violence doesn't work. Constitutional politics make more sense. The great conversion from the bomb to the ballet-box has taken place - we hope. Sinn Féin and the IRA have eventually conceded that peaceful democratic politics is more effective than politically motivated violence and mayhem.

It took thirty years, three and a half thousand deaths, ten thousand injuries, an unquantifiable number of traumatised individuals, the loss of thousands of jobs and the destruction of millions and millions of pounds worth of property. And Sinn Féin, with the arrogant self-confidence that is now their trademark, have done their best to cast it as some kind of victory. It gives a whole new meaning to Seamus Mallon's comment about political slow learners.

There is, of course, another view. It is that Sinn Féin and the IRA haven't experienced a road to Damascus experience. Rather they have recognised that terror is no longer acceptable in post 9/11 America no matter how well it's dressed up by the extremes of Irish America. And they know that the Irish people would no longer tolerate the dual strategy - in Danny Morrison's famous words - of 'the ballot box and the armalite.'

Maybe all this isn't a change of heart for Sinn Féin and the IRA at all. Maybe they've just concluded, in a hard-headed political way, that the armalite would no longer be tolerated by the Irish electorate. It could well be that this is just the ultimate cynical tactic, that all the guff about democracy and constitutional politics is a facade and that the phoenix of armed conflict will rise again if the constitutional path does not reap a presumed harvest. Do leopards ever change their spots?

The overwhelming feeling of relief that the republican movement has at long last recognised the futility of what they called 'armed conflict' has to be balanced by a reasonable question about the wisdom of trusting their word. The Sunday before the final act of decommissioning Sinn Féin organised a united Ireland rally where teenagers carried imitation guns through the streets of Dublin. It may, of course, be just part of a choreographed effort to convince the hard men in the run-up to the deal on policing. Or it could be that the Provos still can't see that for progress to be made in building peace and reconciliation, changes in attitudes and perspective are necessary. Or it may mean that the Provos simply don't believe that 'the war' is over.

Apart from the fact that displaying military symbols is, I imagine, in clear breach of the law – and the Gárdaí blithely escorted the rally through the streets – the message seemed to be that the Provos haven't gone away, you know. What shape or form that continuing presence will have will determine a lot about the possibility of achieving a lasting peace. As will the reports on whether their involvement in criminality has ended.

The next problem is to decommission Ian Paisley. The furtive nature of the destruction of weapons gave Paisley a handy stick to beat the old drum. While no one doubts the integrity of those involved, not least the two clergymen, Paisley pointed out that there are questions remaining as to whether all the arms were decommissioned. In the circumstances this is not an exact science and the numbers tallied with the estimates provided by both governments. But how can we be certain that the Provos didn't retain a few hand-guns? Or get more if they imagine they need them.

It's ultimately about trust. After all that has happened, can we trust the Provos? Paisley consistently said No but then Paisley always said No even though more recently his tune changed . . . At some stage, Paisley has given at least a qualified Yes so it seems now for Paisley that this is it or as s Gerry Adams said, *Sin é*.

But, with respect, it isn't *Sin é*. This is not just about the end game of a political process. It's not just about political institutions. It's about building trust. And that can't be done unless there is some form of what Christians call 'repentance'.

Sooner or later there will have to be an acknowledgement of the hurt caused and a systematic effort to move the healing process forward. What shape or form that will take will have to fit the North's particular requirements. There are so many commemorations, so many marches, so many 'traditions' that it will take a huge effort to shape a path of reconciliation through the maze of conflicting expectations.

But unless that happens the distrust and enmity between the two communities will continue and ensure that, like a huge forest fire that people imagine has been eventually extinguished, smaller fires will continue to flare up spontaneously. The history of republicanism has been that every so often another group breaks off because they imagine that only they have the credentials to carry the flame of republicanism into another generation. For republicans, the first item on the agenda, as Brendan Behan famously remarked, is always 'the split'.

As many people have already remarked, we're not really at the end of anything. At best we're now at the beginning of something. What that's going to be no one can quite tell. But at least we're now going in the right direction after the mayhem and the futility of the last thirty years.

History no doubt will judge the Provos' great achievement as the possibly irreparable damage their campaign has inflicted on the goal of a united Ireland. But, of course, no one could tell them.

Small rural communities that in the past were vibrant parishes are now virtually disappearing as worshippers search out in neighbouring parishes a more convenient time for Mass. If such communities are close to large towns offering a varied schedule of Masses, such small parishes are, in effect, beginning to exist in name only

Disappearing parishes

COMMUNITY, as we used to know it, is dying. Life is becoming more and more private. Money and the spread of choices it brings is creating a different Ireland. We are becoming a different kind of people.

It's not an original point and not everyone pines for the way we were – as it had its shadow side as well. But there's a growing sense that the kind of togetherness that sustained small rural communities is disappearing and that we're living through a strange transition period.

One element in the present mix is the changing pattern of worship. I don't mean just that fewer attend Mass, for example, and the consequent loss of that important community bonding. But that fewer and fewer actually go to Mass in their own parishes. The most important thing about Mass now, someone said to me recently, is the time it's at. What matters for many people now is not the quality of the liturgy or the standard of singing or how pertinent the sermon is but when Mass is on.

Sunday mornings are now full of a series of social and sporting engagements and, for a growing percentage of those who go to Mass, fitting in the Mass around their particular hobbies or whatever is a key strategy. People are prepared to travel up to twenty miles to get a Mass at the right time. And while this doesn't make much difference in a large parish, it can bleed smaller parishes of their very life-blood.

The sort of people who are energised by a series of social or sporting occasions over a weekend are exactly the kind of energised and involved people parishes need. You're left, someone unkindly said to me recently, with those who have nothing else to do on a Sunday morning except go to Mass! The downstream effect will be that most communities will gradually contract, and some parishes disappear.

Of course this is already happening. Small rural communities that in the past were vibrant parishes are now virtually disappearing as worshippers search out in neighbouring parishes a more convenient time for Mass. If such communities are close to large towns offering a varied schedule of Masses, such small parishes are, in effect, beginning to exist in name only. There are not sufficient worshippers to merit a full schedule of Masses or, for that matter, enough work to merit the presence of a priest.

Re-organisation is inevitable. Priests will be redeployed, parishes will amalgamate, the number of Masses will decrease. Parishes with one priest and two Masses may end up with one Mass and no priest. And, of course, if people are not worshipping in their own parishes they're not in a very strong position to object if Masses are discontinued and a parish is closed.

The pattern is very clear. Just as large supermarkets, with a dizzying array of choices, are relegating local shops to a loaf and milk service, large town parishes are doing the same to local churches, sucking in worshippers from rural areas. Without the envelope collection system – where contributions are sent back to the parish of origin of the contributors – rural parishes would quickly become financially as well as pastorally unviable.

But if the logic is that many small parishes are being artificially sustained, there's a point at which declining resources won't allow that indulgence. Priests will be withdrawn, the number of Masses will be curtailed. In modern jargon, cut-backs will be introduced.

What effect this will have on local communities will be an important consideration. Re-organisation may sound the symbolic death knell for some communities: losing first a school, then the post office, now the priest. It's one thing for government cutbacks to curtail the level of services we enjoy in rural areas. It could be the last straw if the Church is seen to plug the plug on a community.

But what choice is there? Now times are different. Priests are getting older; vocations are declining; some parishes are in financial difficulties; the level of services cannot be maintained; two into one won't go.

A start could be made with limiting the number of Masses. Quite apart from any reorganisation of priests, it's becoming more and more obvious that we have too many Masses. Indeed, with smaller populations and greater mobility, we have more Masses now than we had thirty years. Then, the usual pattern was two on a Sunday, one early and one late. That was the choice. Now the vigil Mass has increased that by fifty per cent. Mobility has increased the choice again. Sometimes you can have too many choices!

So what can be done? The first thing might be to cut the number of Masses in each parish. In smaller parishes, one Mass is better than two. One Mass well attended and where the whole effort of priest and people can be directed towards making it the fullest and richest act of community worship possible is obviously preferable to two or three Masses with a small scatter of people in the last few seats of the church. By multiplying Masses, often what we're doing, is just breaking up congregations into small, miserable proportions.

Sooner rather than later a choice will have to be made between providing the widest possible service and creating the optimum circumstances for celebrating Mass in a particular community. What's happening at the moment is that parish boundaries are, in effect, disappearing.

*The Gardaí, like other such groups, are a self-contained body.
Every Garda career started pounding the beat in Templemore and
becoming a Garda meant becoming part of a club that had its own,
often unwritten, rules. There were acknowledged and
unacknowledged rules about what you did and didn't do*

Making our own rules

SOMEHOW it still seems beyond belief. You could understand the shoddy police-work, even the laziness involved, even the basic mistakes that were made, even the breakdown in Garda discipline but something very fundamental was askew when Gardai, in effect, conspired to wrongly accuse people of murder?

This wasn't part of the inevitable slack in a force of twelve thousand men and women. This was crossing a line that policemen should never even contemplate crossing. This was such a fundamental breach of professional ethics that it seems impossible to believe that so many Gardai, at so many levels, conspired to cover it up.

In one way, you might argue, if what was involved was unimportant - a parking ticket or whatever - the instinctive knee-jerk reaction to cover it up, to brazen it out was peripheral enough in the great scheme of things. But the reality here was that two men could have gone to jail for a murder that never happened.

So what went wrong? What emerged from the second Morris Report was that the problems in Donegal emanated from the culture of an Garda Síochána. Morris described it as 'too homogeneous, too inward-looking'.

There's a certain inevitability about that. The Gardaí, like other such groups, are a self-contained body. Every Garda career started pounding the beat in Templemore and becoming a Garda meant becoming part of a club that had its own, often unwritten, rules. There were acknowledged and unacknowledged rules about what you did and didn't do. Not letting down your colleague, even when he was wrong, was just one of them. Whistle-blowing, was unthinkable.

A comparison with the Catholic Church makes the point. Ordination confers not just certain responsibilities but membership of the clerical club. 'The brotherhood of clergy' is an oft-repeated phrase. 'Recreate among priests' is (or was) a common theme. Solidarity with fellow-priests was an accepted part of the clerical code. Not letting the side down, not lifting any stones to examine what might be underneath them were par for the course.

With the child sexual abuse cases in the Catholic church the instinct was to protect one's colleagues. What Morris said about An Garda Síochána could well be said about the clergy of the Catholic Church: 'The monolithic origin of personnel within An Garda Síochána may have contributed to the situation of obstruction involving, as is colloquially said, a circling of the wagons.' The Minister of Justice, Michael McDowell, called it the 'hedgehog' reaction, rolling into a ball and hoping it would all go away. Whistle-blowers, in any professional group, even when they operate from the purest of pure motives, are invariably reviled.

It's what institutions do to protect themselves: banks, politicians, Gardaí, solicitors, clergy. And, then when you-know-what hits the you-know-what, the circling of the wagons is seen as a pathetic attempt to justify the unjustifiable and inevitably the vultures gather.

Circling the wagons contained the situation years ago when people had an unwarranted confidence in bank managers, Garda sergeants and parish priests. Criticism could easily be dismissed. Anyone who persisted was sidelined as a trouble-maker or a communist. Authority was unquestioned and unquestioning.

Now people know better. There isn't an educated elite that tell us what to think. Everyone is educated, if they take the trouble. There isn't anymore an exclusively biddable media converting press releases into what people imagined was news. Instead we have an educated and politically literate people who can tell when a spin is in operation and an effective media who know that real news is what someone somewhere is trying to cover up. And there is the growing sense that it is the whistle-blowers who ultimately insist that professional groups do what they say they do.

There were, it seems, particular problems with the Gardaí in Donegal. Discipline was lax, even to the extent of a Garda on duty drinking with a colleague in a pub. Gardai refusing to say where they were while on duty. Incompetent leadership. And so on. But it would be foolish to imagine that the Donegal situation is unique because the elements that conspired to produce the Donegal scandal - and scandal it is - are present in every other Garda area. The problem isn't the water in Donegal.

As the country gets its breath back after the shocking findings of the second Morris Tribunal Report, it seems clear that we have reached a definitive point in recent Irish history where, once again, a well-regarded institution in Irish life is left picking up the pieces.

What is needed now is a root and branch analysis of what happened and a systematic rebuilding of structures that are accountable and transparent. The message is always the same when such crises arise in the great institutions in Irish life: everyone has to be supervised, everyone has to be accountable to someone. When people start doing what they want from the safety of the club then the situation gets out of hand. That's what happens when power exists without personal accountability: abuse, arrogance and lies.

My sympathies are with the vast majority of decent Gardaí whose authority has been compromised by the failures of a few. But it needs to be sorted. Or it will happen again. Nobody, nobody, nobody should ever feel that they can make their own rules.

Cura is for people who find themselves with an unexpected pregnancy and who have to be counselled calmly, sensitively and non-judgmentally. At the end of the day that young woman or girl, with her boyfriend (or often without her boyfriend) has to be helped, in an accepting and respectful environment, to tease out for herself, for her baby, for her family and friends, the implications of whatever decision eventually emerges

No middle ground

POET-UNDERTAKER Thomas Lynch's, *The Undertaking*, is a stunning memoir full of wisdom, serious and funny at the same time. It's full of insight, the kind of book that as you read it, you keep saying, 'That's it!'

I thought of *The Undertaking* when the recent Cura controversy was raging. In matters of life and death, Lynch writes, there seldom is any middle ground and debate is controlled by the extremes 'each side shouting answers and accusations over the heads of the people in between.'

We know exactly what he means. For example, mention the word 'abortion' in Ireland and what you often get is not debate but name-calling. No one listens. Each side attempts to shout down the other. Accusations are thrown over and back, over the heads of those caught in the crossfire, including those who find themselves in crisis situations struggling to make the right decisions.

Cura is for people like that. People who find themselves with an unexpected pregnancy and who have to be counselled calmly, sensitively and non-judgmentally. At the end of the day that young woman or girl, with her boyfriend (or often without her boyfriend) has to be helped, in an accepting and respectful environment, to tease out for herself, for her baby, for her family and friends, the implications of whatever decision eventually emerges. Megaphone denunciations about abortion simply make that task more difficult.

So what was the problem? Some years ago the government set up the Crisis Pregnancy Agency (CPA), an umbrella organisation of different groups involved in helping those unhappily pregnant. Its function was to help reduce the number of abortions. And a working formula was agreed to help the different agencies function as part of the CPA.

Cura's approach was to present an unhappily pregnant woman with a number of options: to keep her baby, to offer her baby for adoption and so on. Cura, of course, is a Catholic agency so it didn't offer abortion as an option. But if after approaching Cura and being counselled by Cura a young woman decided she wanted an abortion, then Cura would refer that woman to another agency. That other agency, as part of the Crisis Pregnancy Agency, then had a responsibility in law to bring the woman through the different options again and if she still insisted that she wanted to have an abortion then that agency would give her the details about having an abortion.

Cura thought long and hard about whether it could work this approach, because it could (as it has) be suggested that in some way Cura was colluding with abortion. But Cura went with it for a number of reasons. One was that referring a pregnant woman (who had decided she wanted an abortion) to another agency had the effect of slowing down her decision because whatever agency she was referred to had to take her through the whole gambit of choices again. Another was that information on abortion is now readily available anyway but by referring a woman who decided she wanted an abortion to another agency, it had the effect of slowing down the decision. The referral to another agency is a kind of a safety net against fast-track decisions for abortion.

This is not about the Catholic Church facilitating abortion because the Catholic Church, as everyone knows, just doesn't do that. This is not about Cura facilitating abortion because Cura, as a Catholic agency, cannot and has not ever facilitated abortion. This is about devising a pastoral practice that will help slow the decision-making process of a young (mainly), vulnerable (always), frightened (mostly) woman who finds herself unhappily pregnant. This is about working within a system that will help to lessen the prospect and, logically, the number of abortions.

It was easy to say, as some have said including *The Irish Catholic*, which should know better, that Cura were co-operating with abortion, which of course they weren't and had no intention of doing. Cura had taken advice on their policy from a moral theologian; they had reflected on it at some length and they came to the conclusion that they should become involved with the Crisis Pregnancy Agency and with the referral procedure.

And the reason for it wasn't that the government would subsidise Cura if they were involved. The main reason they went with this was that the evidence was that if the decision in a crisis pregnancy situation was slowed down then fewer women actually opted for abortion. The effect of this arrangement was that fewer Irish women in crisis pregnancy situations actually opted for abortion.

What happened was that a few Cura personnel were unhappy with the Cura policy and created a fuss. In response the bishops, afraid that there might be any doubt about the Catholic Church's attitude to abortion, changed the policy. The irony of the whole thing is that even though Cura, in its policy, was lessening the level of abortion, the policy has to be changed even if it, in effect, increases the level of abortion!

I have two fears about the Cura change in policy. One is that we're now going to have an increase in abortions because the new policy of Cura will be less effective than the old policy. The second is the damage all this may do to Cura and the loss that would be to those who avail of their services.

Once again, like in the last abortion referendum, a few extreme people have done enormous damage to the Catholic Church. Who will save us from our simplistic friends?

People like John O'Donohue, who are eventually swamped by a kind of helpless disillusionment with the institutional church, or like John Hegarty, who ultimately reject 'the whole religion thing', are quintessentially 'modern' people who pose awkward but important questions for church and religion.

Small church, little room

WHEN Professor John Hegarty was elected as Provost of Trinity College it got me thinking. Not about Trinity, where by all accounts the Mayo mafia are doing extremely well. Two consecutive Provosts (Tom Mitchell and John Hegarty) and a Chancellor (Mary Robinson). Not bad for Mayo-God-help-us. (Now if we could produce footballers as well as academics we'd be home and dry.) Anyway, it got me thinking not about Trinity but Maynooth.

Hegarty, myself and about eighty others entered Maynooth in 1966 to study for the priesthood. Hegarty left after four years, after a degree in science and a year of theology, much of which by his own admission (to Vincent Browne in an *Irish Times* interview) he spent questioning not just his vocation but religion. I remember it well. Cups of coffee and chocolate biscuits in the college canteen and endless haranguing over the eternal questions. After which, Hegarty concluded that the only way forward for him was 'to ditch the whole (religion) thing'.

I got to thinking: suppose Hegarty hadn't ditched the whole religion thing, hadn't left the seminary. Instead of going to UCG and a Ph.D., further research in the University of Wisconsin, a spell in Bell Laboratories, a professorship in laser physics in Trinity and subsequent election as Provost, suppose he had stayed in Maynooth and was ordained, where I wonder would he be now?

Those unversed in the complex and impenetrable politics of promotion in the Catholic church might suppose that someone like Hegarty - a great mind, a proven leader, a gifted communicator with the common touch, a man at ease with and in tune with the issues of the day - would have made an ideal bishop in today's complex world. While all of that may well be true, the more probable outcome is that Hegarty would now be a curate in Killawalla hoping to be made P.P. of Aughagower in the June changes. Or some such dizzy project. You think I'm exaggerating? Not at all.

Some years ago there were plans, by his diocesan authorities, to appoint the gifted John O'Donohue as a curate somewhere in Connemara. And with all due deference to Connemara curates appointing a semi-genius like O'Donohue to such an undemanding post was the administrative equivalent of the Department of Health appointing the celebrated heart surgeon, Maurice Neligan, as a part-time supervisor in the east car-park of Beaumont Hospital. In the event, O'Donohue claimed a freedom for himself on the margins of an institution that refused to recognise let alone appreciate his enormous talent and is now a best-selling author, a gifted poet and a life-line for many at odds with a church and a liturgy out of time with their needs.

People like John O'Donohue, who are eventually swamped by a kind of helpless disillusionment with the institutional church, or like John Hegarty, who ultimately reject 'the whole religion thing', are quintessentially '*modern*' people who pose awkward but important questions for church and religion. They are in rhythm with the spirit of the age; they submit the questions that surface to an uncompromising intellectual rigour; and they claim a freedom that is at odds with the control and predictability of mainstream Catholic theology. In their world the questions precede the answers.

O'Donohue sold forty-thousand copies of *Anam Chara* in Ireland and more than one-hundred thousand in America not because his readers were beguiled by the hybrid of his discursive analysis of German philosophy - his doctoral thesis in Tubingen was on Hegel - and Irish folk traditions that underpins his best-selling book but because they sense a freedom to dwell on the questions that more under the surface of their lives and a need for a spirituality more personal, more substantial, more satisfying and more intellectually credible than anything the dancing sun of Medjogorje or its equivalents can provide. O'Donohue is popular because in a post-modern world he can converse with contemporary culture. He is in tune with its rhythm.

For example in a recent contribution to *The Irish Times*, Cardinal Desmond Connell stressed the centrality of Christ for the individual and for society but what does that actually men in the lived experience of contemporary Ireland? But who can unpack it or translate it into a language that speaks to the hunger for meaning that is at the heart of a lived life? Where are the O'Donohues who are in rhythm with what's happening in our culture and have the vocabulary to converse with it? Who can open up a path through the complexities and ambiguities of modern life into the rich pastures of our Catholic heritage? Who can respond to the palpable hunger for meaning in our complex world? Who can translate for us?

The difficult truth is that translation of its nature is approximate. And a popular style that communicates in digestible sound-bytes is anathema to those who feel – by personality, training or in deference to the heavy hand of Rome – that they have to ground every utterance in a rigidly orthodox theological framework and in a forest of footnotes. So there is no place, no room for those who can set out a credible and intellectually rigorous stall in the marketplace. And we are left organising flights to Yugoslavia or ferrying reliquaries from post to pillar in an effort, in the immortal words of a former bishop of Meath, 'to horse up a bit of piety'.

No wonder people like Terry Eagleton, the Oxford don, lament the tediously predictable, knee-jerk rejection of Catholicism that passes for a coming of age in Ireland. 'One of the more insidious crimes of the Irish Catholic church' he writes 'has been to deprive the nation of the kind of intellectually challenging and relevant version of Christian gospel which it would cost you something to reject'. Hungry sheep look up and are not fed.

Meanwhile we are left with John Hegarty jettisoning, perhaps too neatly, the whole religion thing and those, like John O'Donohue, who could converse with him and the wider world, pushed inexorably to the margins. To paraphrase Behan: 'small church, little room'.

Maybe we have had too many Bodenstowns, too much remembering and glorifying of the patriot dead. There are, in Irish life, political imperatives but there are moral imperatives too. And surely a moral imperative now is to stop honouring the physical-force tradition of republicanism and turn our faces, firmly and courageously, against the wisdom of the past

Too many Bodenstowns

THE State funeral accorded to Kevin Barry and his nine colleagues gives pause for thought. Not least in terms of the Catholic Church's enthusiastic collaboration. Cardinal Daly - in the absence in Rome of Cardinal Connell and Archbishop Brady of Armagh - did the honours. Should the Catholic Church have allowed itself to be used for political, even party political, gain?

It is, of course, part of the Catholic tradition not to deny the Christian burial rituals to almost anyone. But would it not have been more appropriate if the ten bodies were brought back to their own churches and buried simply and respectfully? Or if the government insisted on a communal Mass, would it not have been more appropriate if it was celebrated by the junior curate in the Pro Cathedral rather than a prince of the Church?

It was, An Taoiseach told us solemnly, about discharging 'a debt of honour'. The Mountjoy Ten's actions had 'legitimacy' – someone explained – 'a mandate' from the results of the 1918 election. Dangerous words those – legitimacy, mandate, honour. The Provos believed that they had 'a mandate' too and John Hume had to devise the cross-border referenda to divest them of that 'mandate', imagined or real. The Real IRA believed that despite the referenda they had a mandate to slaughter people in Omagh, even though Gerry Adams condemned it. And now that the Provos have decommissioned their weapons, other Republican groups will in turn accuse them of betrayal, jut as republicans accused Fianna Fail in the past. And no doubt they will imagine they have a mandate too.

There is a violent, virulent strain of republicanism running like an open sore through Irish history. And periodically it erupts bringing terrible devastation in its wake. Are we going to continue to 'honour' people who were part of a physical force and violent tradition just because there was a vote nearly a century ago? Are we going to continually honour them when we know that to honour them is to honour the tradition and by extension and implication – some will surely feel – to honour those who bombed Omagh? And may be encourage other brave young men to spill more blood for that fourth green field?

This isn't some esoteric political point that makes for an interesting debate to while away the winter. This is a lethal virus in the body politic that has brought death to more than three thousand people in the last thirty years and an incredible degree of suffering to thousands more – injured, traumatised, broken. And we have to be very careful that subtle distinctions, which sometimes demand a certain political sleight of hand, are not lost on those who believe that such words are an encouragement to go out to finish the job of acquiring 'the fourth green field.'

Perhaps it is necessary to say with some force that making distinctions between different strains of republicanism – and analysing in detail who has what mandate from whom or for how long – is unhelpful and that we need, in these hopeful times, to do everything we can to negative the corrosive effect on Irish life of that violent strain of republicanism. If the patriots of the past will forgive us, maybe we have honoured them enough. Maybe we have had too many Bodenstowns, too much remembering and glorifying of the patriot dead.

There are, in Irish life, political imperatives but there are moral imperatives too. And surely a moral imperative now is to stop honouring the physical-force tradition of republicanism and turn our faces, firmly and courageously, against the wisdom of the past.

In those simple days, when we all knew the words of that tedious ballad, *Kevin Barry*, a kind of vague, undiluted patriotism had the wind at its back. The word 'republican' had a decency and an integrity to it. But then came the Troubles and a grim awakening to the reality behind the song. 'Republicanism' lost its sheen.

For thirty years we pushed ourselves through the hoops of violence and death in the name of freedom. We had our Omaghs and our Enniskillens, murder and mayhem among the dreary steeples of Fermanagh and beyond. And then slowly, gradually and inexorably, we saw light at the end of the tunnel, beyond violence and death, a belief that it is possible to achieve opposing political aims if people are prepared to respect the legitimate rights of different traditions.

Jack Lynch tried to give 'republicanism' a lower case 'r'. His party resisted and some of his party, for short-term political gain, remained adept at playing the Republican card. And many brave and foolish young men took them at their word and bought into the republican dogma – the creed that stretched all the way back to Wolfe Tone and that became entangled with 'the fight for Irish freedom'. But when the cost of the last thirty years had been counted and when short-term political game was replaced by the vision of people like John Hume, a new dispensation became possible through the Peace Process: respect, accommodation, partnership.

The next logical step is to say that we have honoured the tradition of republican violence too much for too long. We need to stand back form it and assess the cost of 'freedom' and who paid for it. We need to face down the name-calling that will inevitably ensue. And we need to confront those who for party political gain make cynical speeches about 'the fourth green field'.

What message will other young men take from the State's belated endorsement of Kevin Barry's deed? Are we tilling the soil for republican Bin Ladens to appear on a distant horizon to take life in order to win back the 'fourth green field'? Is it possible to continue to indulge our tradition of violent republicanism without sowing the seeds of bloody conflict for future generations to reap?

Jack is part of a growing subculture in Irish life, caught between those committed in the fullest sense to rearing their children in the faith and those less interested in what baptism means but who accept the social routine. It's not that such parents actually disbelieve in God – though some do.
(That for many is still a bridge too far).

A different country

IN John McGahern's novel *That They May Face The Rising Sun*, set in Co. Leitrim in the Eighties, the following exchange takes place between Jamesie and Ruttledge:

Why don't you go to Mass, then, if you are that low?

What's that got to do with it?

You'd be like everyone else round her by now if you went to Mass.

I'd like to attend Mass. I miss going.

What's keeping you, then?

I don't believe.

None of us believes and we go. That's no bar.

I'd feel a hypocrite. Why do you go if you don't believe?

I read that passage shortly after I had a conversation with a young man - let's call him Jack - whom I knew some years ago. He asked to talk to me about a dilemma he had. He and his wife had recently had a young baby boy and they were both delighted with their young son.

The difficulty was that they didn't want to baptism him. There was huge pressure to have the baby baptised - particularly from the grandparents. But while his wife was prepared to go through with the ceremony just to satisfy everyone, Jack wasn't happy to be bounced into a decision. When he investigated the detail of the commitments he as a parent was expected to make, he felt that it would be hypocritical to promise to rear his child in the faith when he wondered whether he had the faith himself and when, all things considered, he wasn't particularly anxious for his child to have it.

Normally, he said, there would be no dilemma for him. He didn't go to Mass. He had 'got out from under the religious thing' but that didn't mean that wasn't a part of him that wanted to belong. He resented this parting of the ways, this definitive choice, for himself and his son and his mother, who wanted him desperately to baptise her grandchild. If he didn't, he felt she would never forgive him.

Nobody, he said, seemed to understand his dilemma. Everyone does it, Jack was told. It's just a ritual. It's a cultural thing. It's like belonging to a club. There's no alternative. Just say the words but don't mean them. It's an empty formula. It's just a prelude to a great night. You're too precious, too serious, for goodness sake. You're posturing.

Jack is a version of McGahern's Ruttledge, well enough disposed to religion, accepting that it has a value, standing at a distance from it, careful not to disrespect it because to do so would be to disrespect those he love. But he cannot pretend either that it is more than what his experience of it is or that he would want to shape his life around it. He knows that baptism is a serious business, that there are very precise and detailed commitments undertaken by parents in the process, that it's all there in the small print. But it's more than what he wants.

Jack is part of a growing subculture in Irish life, caught between those committed in the fullest sense to rearing their children in the faith and those less interested in what baptism means but who accept the social routine. It's not that such parents actually disbelieve in God - though some do. (That for many is still a bridge too far). Rather they have - as they would see it - a less intense, less specific faith in a less demanding God and are anxious that their children do not have the unrelenting, guilt-ridden, oppressive system of religion that they feel was imposed upon them.

These are parents who sense that they no longer really believe in the Catholic God and don't want to commit themselves to rearing their children in the Catholic faith. Like McGahern's Ruttledge, part of them wants to be at Mass, to do the religious thing, to belong, but they feel it would be hypocritical to pick and choose the bits that suit them, to pretend that they are taking the whole package. They are, in the main, serious people, devoted to their children, with strong moral and ethical beliefs, highly principled in their dealings with others, convinced that there are great benefits for society and the individual in the religious quest but uncomfortable with the Catholic faith to which their parents are often instinctively and absolutely committed. What they want is a spirituality for themselves and their child but they'll pass on the religion, if you don't mind. If there was a secular equivalent to baptism, some naming ritual that would serve as a credible substitute for baptism, and if there was no family or social pressure, it would suffice.

What seems to be happening is that a culture that automatically presumed a religious consensus - is breaking down. The conditioning that instinctively regarded baptism as automatic is being placed under the microscope. And such couples find themselves caught between two different worlds. Casualties of our fractured time.

It's a lonely place to be, that promontory of their own choosing. In a way it's a form of exclusion, voluntarily accepted. Going it alone. Out of sync with the tribe. Ploughing a lone furrow. And trying to shape rituals that connect with the key experiences of life. And in the process jettisoning liturgies that have centuries of thought and wisdom behind them because they carry in their slipstream a narrow view, perceived as arrogant and patronising by citizens of a different world.

Jack and his constituency know the benefits of ritual, the need for a sense of the sacred, the importance of communal assembly, the value of silence, reflectiveness, prayer. Yet they seem doomed to carve out an alternative, and by comparison, tepid spirituality - finding some kind of focus in caring for the environment, eating organic foods, devouring New Age books and voting for the Greens. And what they perceive as the extremism and oppressiveness of religion blinds them to a sophisticated theology that could in theory open up avenues of energy and life to resonate with their experiences but in practice ends up collecting dust on the shelves. What Jack senses is a take-it-or-leave-it attitude. What he gets is an answer to a question he's not asking. The young are beginning to live in a different country. Like McGahern's Leitrim.

Ten years ago 286,000 attended the final stages of the championships in Croke Park. Now the figure is 534,000. Ten years ago television coverage was limited because traditionalists felt that if matches were televised grounds would be empty. Croke Park, a startling achievement at any level, is a monument to the vision and foresight of those who were prepared to dream about the future rather than to indiscriminately replicate the past

Amateur or professional?

MICK O'Dwyer started it with his suggestion that every player in an All Ireland final should get €10,000. But one way or another the diminishing amateur status of the GAA surfaces year after year. It's inevitable really because once traditions - sporting, religious or otherwise - begin to make their peace with a changing world there's no putting the toothpaste back into the tube.

That happened with the Catholic Church when it realised that to preach the Gospel effectively it had to engage with the real world. The great moment was the Second Vatican Council which underpinned that revolutionary change. Inevitably, of course there are refugees from the religious past who insist on living in a make-believe world - and by all accounts too, tetchy and insulting to all who refuse to accept their narrow view. Their static view of tradition and their embarrassingly thin theology give them, predictably enough, an unwarranted confidence even arrogance in their limited views. Canute is their patron saint: trying to keep out the tide of the modern world, rather than learning how to swim.

The great moment in the GAA was the open draw in the All Ireland series. Ten years ago 286,000 attended the final stages of the championships in Croke Park. Now the figure is 534,000. Ten years ago television coverage was limited because traditionalists felt that if matches were televised grounds would be empty. Instead gate receipts have trebled from something over €5 million in 1995 to more than €17 million last year. And Croke Park, a startling achievement at any level, is a monument to the vision and foresight of those who were prepared to dream about the future rather than to indiscriminately replicate the past.

But part of the price you pay for living in the real world is that you have to continually adapt to changing circumstances. Part of the price the GAA will have to pay for the success of the new-style championship and the financial killing being made is to face the question of professionalism.

For some this is unacceptable, unconscionable, a form of heresy. The amateur ethos is part and parcel of the great GAA tradition, a core value to be defended to the death. But the difficult truth for GAA traditionalists is that once you go along the road to answering the demands of the market-place, you find yourself carried along with the commercial tide.

There are a number of realities that need to be faced. Players today have a much shorter shelf-life than in the past. The gruelling training sessions ensure that players will burn out much more quickly. How many significant players are there in their Thirties now? The time commitment is another factor: wives and girlfriends pay a huge price for those who will cheer their husbands and boyfriends when they win but who will often subject them to incredible abuse when they don't. And for what? For living up to the someone else's theory of the glories of the amateur game?

In *The Irish Times* three sports journalists. Keith Duggan, Seán Moran and Tom Humphries, rejected the call for the payment of players with the usual run of emotional cliches about nothing 'electrifying the soul like running out with your county on these September Sundays', the honour of representing your county and the danger of tampering with 'the distinctively parish and county ethos' of the GAA. And commentators like Joe Brolly saying that the GAA is 'the cement of our society' and that we tamper with its amateur status at our peril. And there is a sense in which all of that is true.

But, with all due respect to Duggan, Moran, Humphries and Brolly it's easy for them to talk. After all as sports journalists the first three are well paid for their reporting, and Brolly has a lucrative sideline to his legal work in his television commentaries, inaccurate and curiously inexpert though they invariably seem to be. And the best of luck to the well-paid managers too, some of whom, we're told, are making up to €100,000 a year. And then there are the GAA officials who control the key appointments at county and national level, often for years on end, and take advantage of the considerable perks available to them. Say no more. And the best of luck to them too.

The key point here is that all of that industry is based on the commitment and expertise of players who are continually being lectured at if they ask for any improvement in their conditions. They and their families make incredible sacrafices in time and effort. I've watched Mayo players training on Enniscrone beach and soldiers going to war for life and liberty hadn't to endure such a punishing regime. On wet February Sundays when the dogs should be left in their kennels county players head out into the middle distance, building up their reserves for a mythical victory on a September Sunday and if they don't achieve it they are roundly abused by armchair experts who wouldn't be able to kick snow off a rope, if their lives depended on it.

For amateur status to make sense, everyone would have to be amateur. But John Maughan, John O'Mahoney, Martin Carney, Michael Lyster, Kevin McStay, Colm O'Rourke, Ger Loughnane and the rest of them are not amateur. They function and they get paid because the players play.

The GAA, like the Catholic Church, will have to learn how to live in our brave new world.

Good old John, a few weeks earlier painting the end wall of the office that lovely shade of Celtic Rose with Daisy standing back to survey his handiwork; and now here he was in his own living room with boring magnolia on the walls and his wife and children, ashen-faced and angry, explaining to him the limitations of his future life

Paying the price

JOHN now lives a life outside his own family. A kind of refugee status, he describes it, in his occasional moments of wry regret. Looking back he can't quite believe what's happened to him. There he was, happily ensconced in his comfortable home, a contented relationship with his wife, Mary; as good a friendship with his adult children as he ever expected to have; mortgage finished; university fees and sundry associated charges almost a thing of the past; retirement beckoning; a second home in Bulgaria; a significant car; good health and a nifty handicap in golf. All of that, and heaven too?

John was, indeed is, one of those solid citizen types that make things happen. In community and church he wasn't one for leaving it to others. Whenever something needed to be done, he was there, giving a hand. You could bet your house on him.

Then she arrived. Let's call her Daisy. A young flighty thing. *Bubbly*, I think, is the appropriate word. Her dress was adventurous. Her smile was infectious. Her personality way out there in front of her. And John, as we say in the country, lost the run of himself.

Daisy took the office by storm. Files were tidied away. Pot plants suddenly appeared in every corner. Air freshners materialised in the staff toilet. Little hand-towels replaced the old machine on the wall with that damp, soiled towel hanging dejectedly from it. Windows were opened, literally and metaphorically. And staid, middle-class, stolid, John was smitten.

On reflection he should have known that he had moved off the predictable radar when instead of visiting his aged mother which he did like clockwork every Saturday, he found himself painting one wall of the office a hideous rose colour with Daisy prancing beside him talking about things like colour co-ordination, things which he had never before in his life given a second thought to. But that was Daisy. Bubbly, infectious Daisy.

Then, again as we say in the country, one word borrowed another, and John found himself taking Daisy for a late supper now and again and explaining to her how unhappy he was. There's a certain comic side to this now viewed from the perspective of his present misery, but then it seemed to make some kind of sense. She was a great listener, Daisy was. And John even found himself gilding the lily a bit so that he could enjoy that lovely way she furrowed her brow at his sad life.

Anyway, to make a long story short, a weekend away was organised on the pretence that some important client at the far end of the country needed particular attention and, let's say, Aughrim was lost!

Daisy could have been his daughter and he knew that it was all on the borderline of insanity. He knew he was playing with fire. He knew that he should have known better. But, for some reason, he couldn't extricate himself from what now seems to him a crazy and much regretted episode in his middle years. He wanted, he said in an effort to explain things, a trophy to carry with him into his declining years and when he shared these glad tidings with his friends they just looked at him with undisguised contempt. The bloody idiot.

Mary heard of course, as wives do. Hurt, anger, rejection, humiliation, bitterness – the sad thesaurus of broken relationships. And then she entered into a calm ocean where she found the resolve to put the pieces of her life back together again. But without John.

Good old John, a few weeks earlier painting the end wall of the office that lovely shade of Celtic Rose with Daisy standing back to survey his handiwork; and now here he was in his own living room with boring magnolia on the walls and his wife and children, ashen-faced and angry, explaining to him the limitations of his future life. How could all this have happened?

John now lives in a flat in town. Mary has the house and half his salary, as well as sundry expenses. The house in Bulgaria is under the hammer. He's given up golf. And he has to make an appointment to see his children. He's thinking of moving in with his mother, though he's not too sure about that. Nor is she, though his mother thinks, as mothers do, it's all Mary's fault.

Daisy has moved on, of course, with no appreciation of the unhappiness and devastation her little adventure brought to so many people. No doubt she's painting another office a less than subtle Celtic Rose . . .

What is it about men in this twilight zone? A friend of mine is writing a book about mid-life and he's going to call it *Men who Pause!* Is this some kind of male menopause when all men begin to see is a declining future and can't really cope with the impending reality of death? Is it that life is shutting up shop, a series of avenues are closing down and men need some mad fling to reassure themselves that life isn't passing them by.

John would like to be able to unspool the last few months of his life. To go to Bulgaria with Mary for a few weeks, to welcome his daughter home for the weekend, to experience the precious ordinariness of his former life that once looked uninteresting, even boring. And now seems all he would wish to have.

Worst of all, he knows that he has no one to blame but himself.

Don't believe what you read in the papers

DON'T believe what you read in the papers is sound advice. Because what's in the papers may be anywhere on the spectrum between absolutely true or completely untrue. Or, in these days of spin, calculated to create a perception based on a particular agenda.

Like when the death took place in America of Archbishop Paul Marcinkus. He was the man who was dubbed by the media 'the Pope's bodyguard' because he was - all 6 feet four inches of him - forever by Pope John Paul's side during his trips around the world. Marcinkus was the man who decided that the Pope wouldn't meet the people in Knock on that historic day in 1979, and he was never forgiven for it!

Later Marcinkus was named Chairman of the Vatican Bank. His self-deprecating comment at the time that the only experience he had of money was counting the Sunday collection became embarrassingly prophetic when he became embroiled in a series of scandals that led to the death of a man called Calvi amid rumours that the Italian mafia were involved in the whole sordid enterprise.

Unsurprisingly the star of Paul Marcinkus went into steep decline and after the Vatican protecting him for a few years from the Italian courts he retired quietly to Arizona to play golf.

When Marcinkus died predictably obituaries in the papers focussed on the scandals that surrounded him but *The London Times*, at the tail-end of a considered piece, wrote that Marcinkus had a son by his mistress. Interestingly this came to my knowledge after the obituary had been down-loaded from the internet, photo-copied and passed around. It seemed the final nail in his reputation.

There was, however, one problem. It was untrue. A friend of Marcinkus checked one-hundred and thirty-three obituaries around the world but none contained the allegation. So he rang *The Times* and asked them to substantiate it. The writer of the obituary could produce no evidence and *The Times* corrected it in a subsequent edition.

If the friend of Marcinkus hadn't followed it up; if the obituarist hadn't been asked to back up his words; it would have remained the one detail that would be remembered.

In these hard-pressed times for the Catholic Church, there's a tendency simply to believe whatever allegation is made about priests or religious, no matter how outrageous it may be. As I've written here before there's a commercial aspect to the media hyping up allegations. With the result that the atmosphere is such now that completely innocent people are, in effect, being found guilty before allegations are even investigated. In present circumstances, church-people seem to be forever cast in the role as the bearers of bad news.

Last year the principal of Marino Institute of Education in Dublin resigned amid claims and counter-claims of bullying, etc. The institute is run by the Irish Christian Brothers, a congregation reviled in the media over the last few years. The presumption in the media was that the Christian Brothers had made another grand mess and wouldn't you think that they'd get their act together.

An independent body was asked to investigate and in its report it came down firmly on the side of the authorities. Another conclusion was that some members of staff were running a campaign in the media to wrest control of the college from the Christian Brothers and to get it established as a free-standing teacher-training college.

The college authorities were cleared of the four allegations made against them - unfair treatment, undermining of the college, exclusion of some academic staff from decision-making, intimidation of some staff. In simple terms some staff were unhappy with the structures laid down by the college authorities.

At first the Christian Brothers hesitated to publish the report. Again the presumption was that the report was so embarrassing for them that they didn't want to publish it. Then when the report was published and the authorities came out unscathed, an effort was made to rubbish it in the media as 'not independent'.

What is making it difficult, if not impossible for the Catholic Church to get a fair hearing now in Irish society is the context in which we now seek to survive. There is for example a case to be made that, in present circumstances, priests who are accused of child sexual abuse will not get a fair trial. And regardless of innocence or guilt, reputations are lost anyway. What this perception is creating is an atmosphere of vulnerability and threat around clergy that is having the effect of not just denting our confidence but placing us in an unenviable shadowland.

Added to this is the growing belief among priests that bishops, on the run from the media, are being panicked into forwarding to the authorities bizarre and unsustainable allegations that other groups would simply discount as unworthy. Priests are beginning to feel that, because of past failures by priest abusers and past incompetence by bishops and superiors, that they will end up as victims too. It is not a nice place to be.

Paper won't refuse ink. Gossip, like *Move Over Butter*, will always spread. And often it matters little whether something is true as long as it's a good story. Like the mythical son of Archbishop Marcinkus. Or the mythical allegations of bullying and harrassment by the Christian Brothers. What fits the the prevailing mood may sound right. Or it may be completely untrue.

Don't believe what you read in the papers.

Applause is instinctive. It's an automatic response of appreciation. So when someone sings beautifully in church, an instinctive response is to clap. The difficulty is that this is to misunderstand the function of the contribution that singing makes to liturgy. Singing is a form of praying. And to applaud an individual singer makes the individual contribution more important than the main thrust of the worship

Applause in church

ONCE you knew when you were in a church. People talked in stage whispers. Stillness, solemnity, a prayerful attitude were taken for granted. Adults almost tip-toed to their seats. Children were shushed into silence. It wasn't just the respect there was for the reserved presence of the Blessed Sacrament. There was a quiet and silent ambiance that you felt it was somehow disrespectful to challenge. There was an aura of sacredness that was, in every sense, sacrosanct.

We've lost much of that. Partly through the new liturgy: Mass becoming more accessible to the people (in the vernacular, priest facing the people); liturgy less formal, less rigid; Mass said in locations other than the church; more people involved in ministries like reading and distributing Communion; more movement. And partly through the tenor of our times when there's less respect for tradition, less sense of the sacred and possibly less faith.

As a result the Church as a sacred place has lost much of its aura. It has become in many respects just another building where people gather for a specific purpose. Now people talk in church as if they are gathering for a meeting. They wait for the remains to be brought for a funeral or for the bride to come and rather than be encouraged by the atmosphere of the church to spend time in prayer, they often just chat to pass the time. Indeed very few churches are now what we might call 'prayerful.'

There are advantages and disadvantages to the growing informality of Churches and liturgy. As we've gradually opened up our churches and our liturgies to the world, trying as we do to connect the lives we lead with the way we worship, there are gains and losses. A loss certainly is when the sacredness of the liturgy is compromised by something which is more appropriate at the end of the liturgy or even outside the church. Like applause in church.

Applause is instinctive – at football matches, concerts, wherever people gather. It's an automatic response of appreciation. So when someone sings beautifully in church, an instinctive response is to clap. The difficulty is that this is to misunderstand the function of the contribution that singing makes to liturgy. Singing is a form of praying. When we sing, we pray twice, someone memorably said. So song is part of the seamless garment liturgy is supposed to be with everyone involved, everyone making a contribution. And to applaud an individual singer or indeed a choir in an automatic way breaks up the liturgy and makes the individual contribution more important than the main thrust of the worship. Imagine a congregation clapping a reader! Or the servers! Or the lay ministers! It has the effect of breaking the movement and rhythm of the liturgy.

The point here is that while liturgy has some of the elements of drama – story, stage effect, music – involvement in the liturgy is not a staged performance as in a play or a concert. And to take one element of the weave of liturgy and to applaud it for itself gives the performance a significance beyond what it has and even turns it into something it is not. Applause during Mass, for instance, should be unthinkable. It is inappropriate, disruptive and an indication that those involved don't really understand what's going on.

On the other hand, when the liturgy is over it is appropriate and to be expected that those involved be thanked for their contribution. And indeed that applause should follow if that is the response of the congregation. But there's all the difference in the world between that kind of measured and appreciative response at the end of the ceremony and clapping during the Mass.

Liturgy is prayer and those who sing are helping us to pray better not performing for the public in expectation of a clap, sometimes it has to be said initiated by an enthusiastic relative! Imagine what Mass would be like if every time someone read, sang, carried up the gifts or gave out Communion we had applause instigated by an admiring relative. Moreover the contribution of an individual singer or a choir loses its effectiveness and even its function when it is followed by applause.

These words could provoke a negative response not least from those who believe that thanking people in church has gone, as the saying goes, 'beyond the beyonds.' The point is that contributions to the liturgy are for the sake of the liturgy and not for the satisfaction or the notice of the contributors. We need to focus in on service rather than appreciation.

It's a fair point. Mass is prayer not entertainment. And while we work towards a liturgy that engages people's interest we have to retain a reflective ambiance and a prayerful spirit as effective and essential parts of the vocabulary of our worship. The primary focus in liturgy is on connecting with people at a serious level. Not entertaining the troops.

Maybe what we need before Mass is someone who introduces the Mass by pointing to a few important truths: the Church is a sacred place, Mass is a sacred event, there's a 'crying chapel' to the left hand side of the sanctuary, please turn off your mobile phones and if you are particularly moved by some aspect of the proceedings, no applause in church please.

> *McGahern acknowledged Catholicism as the most important influence on his life and would resist efforts of interviewers to get him to condemn the Catholic Church. He understood the force of ritual, the depth of tradition, the richness of the Catholic heritage and, he could distinguish all of that from the petty nay-sayers who contrive to present Catholicism as a negative, oppressive cultic experience that lacks breadth and depth and richness*

Making grief tender

WE all hope, I think, that as we age we will mellow into people like John McGahern: warm, decent, serene people who can accept the hand that life has dealt us. People who can live and let live, be and let be. Even those of us who may be unlikely candidates for serene old age can recognise the real thing when we see it. Particularly the respect, dignity and graciousness that underpin it.

McGahern was the real thing. A gifted writer, forever refining and re-tuning his sentences, until they hummed with clarity and simplicity. 'It is a writer's job' he said one time 'to look after his sentences. Nothing else.' And he did that, devoting his life to them. It took him twenty years to write *Amongst Women*, now widely regarded as his greatest novel, and the finished work was just a third of the original novel. And his wonderful *Memoir* received the same treatment, forensically pared down until it reached its acknowledged perfection.

People imagined, I think, that it was because McGahern was a naturally shy, retiring man who seemed ill at ease in public that he avoided the public stage. But the truth was that he felt so assured of his ability, so easy with his 'vocation' (as he described it) as a writer that he didn't need to be constantly on television re-assuring the nation about his genius, like some of our less talented writers.

But apart from his writing, at a human level, McGahern was the goods too. His mother – warm, generous and loving – died when he was eight and he and his siblings became the reluctant recipients of his father's uneven care. McGahern's father was a difficult and often violent man who couldn't relate to his children and who, for whatever reasons, disparaged, manipulated and abused them. Other writers, as some have done, would have whined incessantly about their miserable childhoods but McGahern simply told the story and moved on.

Again when his novel, *The Dark*, was banned he didn't protest. Or even appeal the decision. What upset him most. it seemed, was that it made the country seem foolish. When Archbishop John Charles McQuaid insisted that he be sacked from his teaching job because he entered an irregular union, he accepted the decision apparently without rancour. Later he was to forgive McQuaid saying that every time he passed a school and saw the teachers' Volkswagons parked outside he would 'say a silent prayer of thanks to John Charles'. And when his union, the INTO failed to support him, he accepted that too. Later he would retell, in his wry, off-hand way, an encounter with the INTO official. The official upbraided McGahern telling him that 'we could have got over the auld book but what had you to go off and marry the foreign woman for, and thousands of Irish girls with their tongues out for a man'.

Later he would acknowledge Catholicism as the most important influence on his life and would resist efforts of interviewers to get him to condemn the Catholic Church. And even though, in the end, he didn't believe in any formal sense he requested a funeral Mass and the Rosary to be said the clay was being filled in on his coffin.

McGahern had the breadth of vision and the generosity of spirit not to confine his understanding of Catholicism to the personality of a local priest. He understood the force of ritual, the depth of tradition, the richness of the Catholic heritage and, with consummate ease, he could distinguish all of that from the petty nay-sayers both inside and outside the Church who contrive to present Catholicism as a negative, oppressive cultic experience that lacks breadth and depth and richness. Throwing off the trappings of religion would be for McGahern the equivalent of denying, as he put it, 'the weather of his childhood'. Denying himself the culture of Catholicism because of the limitations of the clergy would be, for McGahern, the equivalent of refusing to eat meat because he fell out with the butcher.

Yet there was in McGahern an unswerving commitment to the truth of things. He came at life along a seemingly narrow lane with a quietness, a formality, a calmness and a deceptive simplicity. But in his acute observation he was, in effect, lifting stones and inviting us to examine what lay beneath them. In *The Dark* he invited us to see the spectre of child abuse in Irish life, twenty years before television programmes trumpeted its debilitating presence. And of course he was reviled for it. Later in life he was amused, as he told Eileen Battersby of *The Irish Times* 'that his despairing honesty, once considered a crime of betrayal, had become a badge of honour'.

His great themes were death, suffering, pain and the loss of faith, of hope, of love, what Declan Kiberd called 'the mystery of our presence in the world'. And he worked them through thirty-four short stories, six novels, a play and a memoir.

My own favourite was his last book, *Memoir*, where all the themes that he had worked and re-worked during his life were pushed through the sieve of his own personal experience. The loss of his mother, of course, was the defining experience of his life and he felt that loss all his days. What struck me about this book was that he was able to make grief tender, letting it mellow in the crucible of his own pain.

He will be missed because we need people like him to help us understand who we are.

I get a sense that community no longer really exists. At least not in the traditional sense of a necessary engagement with those who live around us. Progressively people live in different worlds that scarcely impinge on each other. Shopping, going to Mass, different forms of recreation are all moveable feasts. Whatever community now exists takes the form of a gathering around a shared experience like work or sport or school.

Small world

I rarely venture to Dublin now. Too much noise, too much traffic, too much hassle. On the rare occasions when I visit our capital city, to tell the truth, I can't wait to get out of it. After furiously negotiating the inner city, getting on the M50 and heading west is always a kind of liberation. Like the summer holidays from school. You've successfully seen the back of something.

Back home the view is different. And more limited. A series of writing commitments means that I spend more time knocking out words on my computer and looking into my front garden for inspiration. Until recently the view was a deep green. A green lawn extended out in front of me. An overgrown hedge cascaded over a perimeter wall. Swallows dipped and dived and a neighbour's cat loitered with intent around the place. I sense now, since I've left it behind me, how this small part of God's earth could have become my whole reality.

It depends, of course, on the view. Where you are and what you do become your reality. What exists is whatever happens within the limits of our horizons. In some sense we may possess our worlds: at a deeper level our worlds possess us.

A child no more than eight years old sits on a piece of cardboard on O'Connell Bridge, holding out a white plastic cup with a few coins in it. Her eyes devour passers-by as if demanding their involvement in her world. Or at least some of their money. An African shabbily dressed and pulling furiously on a long cigarette stands at the corner of a pharmacy near the GPO and looks into the middle distance. A man who looks like a business executive talks into a mobile phone as he tries to hail a taxi. Same place, different worlds. Same view but the perspective is different.

I get a sense that community no longer really exists. At least not in the traditional sense of a necessary engagement with those who live around us. Progressively people live in different worlds that scarcely impinge on each other. Shopping, going to Mass, different forms of recreation are all moveable feasts. Whatever community now exists takes the form of a gathering around a shared experience like work or sport or school.

We used to hear stories of people living in housing estates in Dublin and not knowing that someone had died three doors away from them. Now people can live cheek by jowl in the country and don't know their neighbour's name. Or who lives in the house next door. Visiting a neighbour's house (or 'rambling' as it is known) has - in the space of a few years - transformed itself from neighbourly interest into an invasion of privacy, an infringement on people's space. Our horizons are narrowing as we create smaller and more private worlds.

I remember once in New York visiting friends. Outside the ground-floor apartment, the street was so busy that we had to park a few hundred yards away in an underground carpark. Cars whizzed by continuously, strange-looking people smoked unusual looking cigarettes and beamed or scowled at passersby. It wasn't a place where you'd stop for a chat to while away the day. It certainly wasn't a place to linger at night.

Inside the apartment a different world existed. A small bit of Ireland with a large Mayo influence (including a copy of the *The Western People*) conspired to convince you that you were at home. There was even a back garden with a lawn, some cherry trees in delicious bloom, walls covered in ivy and a decking area with an overhang to provide what privacy there was among the high-rise building. And yes, we had

217

bacon and cabbage for dinner. The distance between two very different worlds was just a wall.

That New York scene is being replicated all over Ireland. Individual interests are beginning to dictate the pattern of life and by extension the contacts that people have with one another. If you are a member of a golf club or go to Mass (or don't go to Mass anymore) or work as part of a team then most of your life becomes focussed around the people you know and the activities you participate in. Our allegiance is to a progressively narrower interest. And it takes something like a death in the family or Mayo playing in the All Ireland final or the Pope coming to Ireland to re-assert even for a time our allegiance to a wider world.

Meanwhile more of us are spending more of our lives focussing on a narrow garden outside a window that is in danger of becoming our whole reality and the rest of the world a distant place which, like Dublin, we hope we may never have to visit.

The resilience of the quasi-religious artifacts that continue to surface in our lives contain a message of sorts. Much of it, I think, has to do with a direct appeal to the senses. In the old days the Sacred Heart picture dominated our kitchens. The colour and literalness of the Stations of the Cross coupled with the aura that chanting and incense gave our liturgies, helped to answer the need for a tangible religion

The open fire

WATCH a group of people gather in a room with an open fire and instinctively they're drawn to it. Even if the room is warm, even if the fire is merely ornamental, people invariably drift towards it, often holding open their hands towards it in a warming gesture.

Deep inside the human psyche there is an experience that resonates with that pull of the open fire. That resonance probably goes back to a far-distant primitive time when our ancestors gathered to warm themselves around the village fire.

Could a similar resonance be at work in the continued popularity of some religious artifacts today? For instance, candles are everywhere: small, big, fat, thin, simple, decorative, cheap, expensive. People now light candles in their homes: at meals, on side-tables, beside where the fire used to be. Nobody seems able to explain the popularity of candles but it has something to do about reassurance, support, comfort, wholeness.

Incense too is popular. People buy little sticks of it and they light it with the candle to create a distinctive ambiance, to give an aura. Chants of various kinds are increasingly popular as well, even the old Gregorian chant is making a bit of a comeback. And fasting is back in fashion too. Not of course for spiritual purposes but for health, beauty, wholeness and for that special aura that people seek, that feeling of things coming together in their lives. It's as if a quasi-household liturgy is replacing the more formal liturgy of the assembled parish.

In one way, the Sacred Heart lamp in the kitchen and fasting for a spiritual motive can seem peculiarly old fashioned nowadays. And yet, in another way, seeping out of the recesses of our lives is a yearning for an iconography that gives us a rootedness, a sense of ourselves, a connection with the sources that give life meaning.

The resilience of the quasi-religious artifacts that continue to surface in our lives contain a message of sorts. Much of it, I think, has to do with a direct appeal to the senses. In the old days the Sacred Heart picture dominated our kitchens. Statues dominated our churches. The colour and literalness of the Stations of the Cross coupled with the aura that chanting and incense gave our liturgies, especially Benediction, helped to answer the need for a tangible religion.

The enduring popularity of devotions like the ashes on Ash Wednesday, kissing the cross on Good Friday, the blessing of throats on St Blaise's day attest to the need for a less intellectual, more sensual approach to faith and liturgy.

The resilience of the old devotions has surprised those who distrusted what they dismissed as sentimentality but which, in effect, served as conduits of popular spirituality. The effort to usher in a more cerebral, biblical spirituality often left people floundering. In a article in *The Furrow*, Salvador Ryan puts it well when he writes: 'Devotion without doctrine may be mere sentiment but equally, doctrine without devotion remains lifeless'.

Ryan tells a story about a woman in Skopje, Macedonia, who wished to pray that she might have a child. There are only two Roman Catholic churches in Skopje, the cathedral and a small wooden building. First she visited the cathedral and searched out the statue of the Blessed Virgin. As she was about to pray that she might conceive a child, she realised that the Virgin wasn't holding a child but had her two hands down by her sides. It was a statue representing the Immaculate Conception. Once the woman realised that she muttered, 'You're no good to me!' before leaving the cathedral to go to the little wooden church where she found a statue of the Madonna and Child.

Some might hold their hands up in horror at the literalness, even tackiness of that story. Others may smile patronisingly to themselves about the lack of theological refinement. Yet, it's about connection. It's about representation. It's about 'popular' spirituality – popular in the sense 'of the people'. It's about communicating as we normally communicate with voice and sight and touch and feeling.

Could it be that a need for the visual, the tangible, the sensual is not been met in our liturgy and our human need for it is seeping out of the church and re-inventing itself in individuals sitting in their apartments lighting candles, burning incense, listening to chants and hugging plants – an experience not all that different from Benediction!

The answer is not to turn back the clock and re-invent Benediction but to listen to the signs of the times. Ryan's belief is that we need, not so much to return to the past but to rediscover the richness of the tradition and re-invent it anew. What matters is not whether something is replicated from one parish to another or from one century to another but whether it has meaning for people now.

I'm continually amazed at how individuals remark that certain liturgies that left me feeling cold and empty have moved them at an very basic level. I think we need to listen very closely to what people want, what people like because when it works it's resonating with something deep within them.

Because just as its almost instinctive to open our hands to a fire (even when there's no heat coming from it!) we need to tap into the deeper recesses of our consciousness to find the ache for God and the things of God buried within. The unsatisfied hunger is an ache for things spiritual.

While most people strive mightily to explain themselves in a few words, it sometimes appears as if Bertie Ahearn weaves a tapestry of thousands of words that at the end of the day seem to defy any kind of clarity. Once he could talk at length without giving anything away; now he has mastered the art of talking endlessly without saying anything at all.

Loans, gifts and other dilemmas

AS always language was the first casualty. When is a loan, a gift? When is a gift, a loan? When is a minister of government not a minister of government? Are you right (or at least not wrong) when you manage not to violate any ethical guidelines, even when what you did is not right? Or appropriate? Or is it okay, even if the behaviour is not acceptable, when it's just a matter of bad judgement? Is everything acceptable as long as it can be squeezed around ethical guidelines, tax implications and political propriety?

Watching the Dáil exchanges on Bertie Ahern's acceptance of 'loans' from his friends and 'gifts' from his acquaintances, I thought of some of the old dilemmas in Canon Law where the casuists came into their own. If a rabbit in my field standing exactly half-way on the fence was shot by a third party and fell into my neighbour's property, who owned the rabbit? It wasn't so much that the answer mattered as that each side could muster a reasonable argument to support their own view.

I've always regarded Bertie Ahern as a genius. Despite the fact that he was at the centre of the Haughey years while all around him fell like nine-pins and lost their reputations, Bertie seemed to have miraculously escaped any serious accusation of wrong-doing. And even though there was the little matter of pre-signing cheques and giving them to Haughey to do with as he pleased, somehow Bertie's successful depiction of himself as the common man, drinking a pint of Bass in his local pub in Drumcondra, made it seem okay. Sure, you know yourself, these things happen. The anorak persona seemed to make his mistakes understandable and forgivable.

And on the occasions when he had to explain himself, his genius with language rescued him. While most people strive mightily to explain themselves in a few words, it sometimes appears as if Bertie weaves a tapestry of thousands of words that at the end of the day seem to defy any kind of clarity. Once he could talk at length without giving anything away; now he has mastered the art of talking endlessly without saying anything at all. You can never quite know what he's saying or not saying and his rejoinder, if he's losing the argument, is invariably to turn on his opponent and say something like 'Isn't that what I'm saying!' It's a bit like the mystery of the Trinity. Or a bar of soap. You think you've got a grip on it and it's gone again.

Did Bertie do wrong? Yes, he did. In comparison to Haughey's creative accounting, or Liam Lawlor's shufflings, Bertie's wrongdoing is a mere peccadillo. But he took money and he shouldn't have. Anything that compromises, or is seen to compromise, confidence in the office of Taoiseach and the government damages the body politic. We know enough now about brown envelopes and corporate donations and influence on policy-making to be hyper-critical of any public representative, not least a Minister for Finance or a Taoiseach, who might even appear to be going down that road.

Should he have resigned? Probably not. It was a misjudgement and on balance Bertie didn't deserve to be shunted ignominiously into premature retirement. And he needs to be there to nurse the North through its next crisis when it comes. And he apologised to the Irish people. But he should have said he had done wrong.

'Right' is not about not being able to be accused of 'wrong'. Right, in this case, is recognising that there should be no gap between public duty and private interest. And no gap between being a minister and a private individual, when it comes to accepting money, as gifts or loans or anything else.

Has the office of Taoiseach being damaged? Yes it has. Has politics being damaged? Yes it has because everytime an office-holder compromises himself or herself, or even appears to be compromised, then the office they hold is damaged.

There's an old-fashioned kind of honour that seems to have faded out of politics. It had to do with an exaggerated sense of propriety that's the other end of the spectrum from self-justification. Or context. Or, in Michael McDowell's word, 'proportionality'. Or shuffling our way in by the side of this code or out by the side of that requirement. It had to do with the protection of institutions which underpin our democracy and there could be no suggestion of compromise. The problem with politics is that, in a world of compromise, core-values can easily lose their sheen.

The best way to test any form of behaviour is to apply it to approximate examples. I might be impressed with my local Garda Sergeant but it always felt wrong giving him a turkey for Christmas. I might have great respect for my local judge but offering him a holiday in the sun?

We lose contact with what's appropriate, if what's not appropriate becomes the norm. Like appointments to state boards and offices. In the Dáil Bertie Ahern commented that he had appointed people to state boards, not because they had given him money, but because 'they were friends.' Interestingly, the opposition parties made little of this. Probably because, if there was a change of government, they would feel entitled to appoint their own cronies to the same boards.

An abuse that's obvious to everyone in Ireland, apart from politicians. Will Enda and Pat change it? No, they won't.

Isn't it wonderful that children are so happy on their First Communion day? Isn't it reassuring that parents enter into the whole experience with them and give them such support? Isn't it great that such an effort is made to make the day special? And isn't it all, or most of it, a compliment to First Communion?

Excess or celebration?

EVERY year, smack in the middle of the First Holy Communion season, there's a dreary debate about what's wrong with it: the excess that's associated with it; the cost of it; the fact that those who can least afford it spend most on it; that it's more a social occasion than a religious event. And so on.

You get the feeling that somewhere in the bowels of every national newspaper's library there's a fat file with the words *First Communion* written on it that is taken out and dusted at the appropriate time every year. And in it are apt quotations from all the usual suspects, right across the spectrum, from the pious to the non-believing, all suitably offended by the excesses of a modern First Holy. All that's needed is some example of a seasonal craziness to put an edge on the copy.

In a recent *Sunday Tribune* Fiona Looney relates an incident that happened at a First Communion ceremony in a Dublin parish two years ago. As a little girl placed the Communion in her mouth for the first time, her father, sitting in the congregation, pressed a remote control device and the child's tiara suddenly lit up in a particularly glorious display of lights that almost knocked the priest down. And *The Irish Times* recently devoted a full page to the First Communion phenomenon. Reading it you felt someone said: It's the season; it needs to be marked; let's get the file out again. The focus of these worthy pieces is always on excess. A list is made out of the how expensive the day can be with outrageous price lists attached. So much for the hair-do, the Communion dress, tiara, stole, parasol, cape, the self-tanning cream and a list of novelties from bouncy castles in the back garden to huge meals in hotels. And then there are the new outfits for the parents . . . Write that up in a jolly, fun way, put in a few comments about First Communion children collecting a small fortune from their hard-pressed relatives and the file can be put away for another year.

But there's nothing in these articles on what First Holy Communion is all about. Nothing about the religious significance of individual children taking another step along the road of faith, another stage of a faith journey. No sense of the expectation and promise built up over the whole year. Nothing about First Confession or what happens in school. Nothing about the part parents play in the preparation. Nothing about the great parish occasion it is.

Yes, there are lots of comments about First Communion as a social ritual, as a rite of passage, as a great family occasion. There are even comments that in some sense it isn't really a religious event at all – because children at such a young age are not really capable of entering into the significance of the occasion.

But that's to ignore the extraordinarily dedicated and nuanced work that teachers do in preparing children; it's to ignore a religious programme that meets children where they are and that works out of their own experience; it's to ignore the religious significance that a parish and the wider community bring to the experience of First Communion day.

But all that religious significance mightn't go down that well with the burgeoning subculture in Irish life that insists that religious faith and the expression of that faith should be catered for in private rituals behind closed doors. Teasing out what First Communion means in religious terms or analysing the sources of a changing but rooted religious faith in our culture might make more sense but doesn't make good copy. So all we're left with are the seasonal cliches about the faintly scandalous co-existence of fake tans and receiving First Communion.

I remember once in my innocence recommending at a parents' meeting that an effort should be made to tone down what I dismissed as the secular frivolities that threatened to swamp the religious significance of First Holy Communion: the cost, the accessories, the clothes, the meals, etc. Afterwards a father took me to task about my attitude. There was, in his opinion, no contradiction between the religious event and celebrating that event in style. It was one of the great significant occasions of his daughter's life and his family, unused to eating out, was going to mark that occasion by having a lovely meal in a restaurant. Why shouldn't it be celebrated? Why shouldn't his family buy new clothes to mark this great event? Why should we have a view of religion that tended to equate misery with holiness?

He was right, of course. And the begrudgers, like myself, with our narrow view, were and are wrong. I accept that now. Isn't it wonderful that children are so happy on their First Communion day? Isn't it reassuring that parents enter into the whole experience with them and give them such support? Isn't it great that such an effort is made to make the day special? And isn't it all, or most of it, a compliment to First Communion?

Someday, like Napoleon, they too will remember their First Communion day as full of happiness and joy. Isn't that what God wants it to be too?

Speed and dangerous driving have not just a ferocious grip on a huge percentage of the male population but also the implicit support of most of the rest of the male population. It would be impossible, for example, to garner any support for mechanically ensuring that cars are incapable of doing more than, say, seventy mph. It seems a logical thing to do. If there is no road in Ireland where the law permits you to go over seventy mph what's the point of having a car that can do twice that?

Men and cars

I REMEMBER a psychologist talking once about human development. He made the point that sometimes, for whatever reasons, some parts of our brains develop more slowly than others, with the result that you can have different levels of maturity in different areas in the same person. One part of the brain develops normally; and, for some unknown reason, the development of another part of the brain becomes arrested.

That may explain fanatical devotion to Manchester United - of course, this doesn't apply to Liverpool fans - but how can we explain the almost exclusively male interest in cars and speed? What is it about some - many - mature men who seem to lose the run of themselves completely when it comes to cars? What is it about the car that induces such testosterone-fuelled immaturity once a man, almost of any age, gets behind the wheel?

What part of the under-developed male psyche is missing that a souped-up car is needed to supply the deficit?

There are, of course, a number of theories some of which couldn't be mentioned in a dull column like this. But the extraordinary thing is that a sizeable percentage of the male population never successfully out-grow what to many seems an adolescent compulsion. In one sense, it's easy to under-stand why young men, full of angst and insecurity, drive low cars at impossible speeds and seem to imagine that this earns them brownie points with their girl-friends and attention, if not admiration, from the mature population.

Invariably, I imagine, their girl-friends just put up with their immaturity as a price to be paid for their dangerous company and their elders just hope that they'll grow up before killing themselves or someone else.

But what about their fathers and grandfathers - steady, dependable, outwardly mature citizens - belting along at ridiculous speeds for no other reason than that there's an open road in front of them and an accelerator under their foot?

Speed and dangerous driving have not just a ferocious grip on a huge percentage of the male population but also the implicit support of most of the rest of the male population.

It would be impossible, for example, to garner any support for mechanically ensuring that cars are incapable of doing more than, say, seventy miles per hour. It seems a logical thing to do. If there is no road in Ireland where the law permits you to go over seventy mph what's the point of having a car that can do twice that?

Yes, of course, it's about freedom but hands up all those with one-hundred and forth miles per hour cars who travel at that speed in the privacy of their own property. Yet we permit thousands of cars on the public roads which do that every day in order to facilitate this mythical personal freedom when exerting that freedom means that some teenager, the apple of his or her parents' eye, will be buried next week as a result.

Why is it that people who manage to break the speed limit and not get caught receive such public acclamation?

Why is it that motorists who see Garda checkpoints in operation imagine that it's some kind of collective civil responsibility to warn oncoming traffic and to facilitate the breaking of the law? And in effect, make it more likely that innocent are killed on the roads?

The BBC television series, *Top Gear*, which worships the motor-car, recently threw up an interesting commentary on the public's obsession with cars. Richard Hammond, the presenter, sustained a brain injury during a three-hundred miles per hour crash and made a full recovery. News of the crash was greeted with a strange admiration for such dare-devil machismo. A more balanced view is that Hammond, who is thirty-six and the father of two young daughters, is an irresponsible idiot placing his own life and the life of his daughters at great risk. But because he was living out a middle aged fantasy - for the titillation of middle-aged car fanatics - such irresponsibility receives some kind of street credibility. We do that all the time. Someone announces that he left Dublin at nine o'clock and he was having a cup of tea in Ballina at eleven-thirty pm and he expects us to gasp in admiration at his achievement when we should be locking him up as the insane fool he is.

Or car fanatics who resent any Garda interference with their right to drive irresponsibly on the roads ring up *Liveline* to complain about speed limits and we indulge them by actually listening to their nonsense when they should be banned from the airwaves.

Or we look with curious indulgence on boy-racers, on their way to an almost certain rendezvous with death - their own or someone else's - when we should be reporting them to the Gardai who should seek them out and get them permanently off the road, for their own safety and for everyone else's.

There is, of course, no political will to come to terms with speeding on the roads. Predictably the Enda and Pat bandwagon didn't take on this killer in our midst as part of their political platform in the general election. It's just too unpopular. So we're going to have to continue to pay a huge price for the old motorcar and the freedom we continue to give male fantasists to kill their fellow-citizens.

What the anti-religionists refuse to do is to seriously debate the contribution of religion to the individual life and to a wider society. The failures of proponents of religion are often all too clear, the achievements often hidden. Everyone knows what priests and religious did wrong; how many know or think about or even care about what they did right? Unless it's on television, someone said recently, it doesn't exist.

Assumptions and delusions

YOU hear it all the time now, the snide remarks about religion. Once people wore their religion on their sleeves as a badge of honour, as a way of establishing a degree of credibility for what they had to say. Now you find the opposite. 'I've no religious beliefs myself, of course' people say on radio, implying that they've now reached a point of pure enlightenment, somewhere beyond the dreadful foothills of superstition. Or 'I was brought up a Catholic myself, but I've left all that behind me', as if it was some dreadful rash that took years to clear.

Richard Dawkins, author of a series of books debunking religion, has brought this trend to a new level and debunked the very idea of God. God, he says, in his latest book, is a delusion. It doesn't help his case all that much to try to prove that a God whom very few people actually believe in doesn't exist. Or that he imagines debunking the traditional proofs for the existence of God (which have been debunked by intelligent believers for years) proves his case. Or that he uses his status as a scientist to establish his credibility when other scientists of equal stature happily question his conclusions.

What is extraordinary about people like Dawkins is the absolute certainty they bring to their belief in the non-existence of God. The onus, it seems, is on believers to prove God exists rather than on unbelievers to prove he doesn't. And of course the notion that you can prove or disprove God from science is a bit like saying you can prove or disprove someone loves you. You may have good reasons for believing in God (or believing in love) but there is a point at which a step of faith has to be made. And that's just as true of non-belief.

Part of the difficulty is that religion often does itself no favours. From the Crusades to Al-Quieda to scandals in the Catholic Church, there's plenty of evidence to support a productive vein of criticism of established religions. The other point is that religion, unlike journalism or science or medicine, demands of its practitioners a very high standard as if bad practitioners discredit religion the way a bad teacher, for example, doesn't discredit education. Or the way awkward butchers don't turn people off meat.

Of course, as surely as there is a religious fundamentalism, there is an anti-religion fundamentalism too. And both fundamentalisms refuse to posit any credibility in the opposite side. You see shades of this in some journalists who never seem to have a good word to say about religion or church and who seem almost to salivate in anticipation of any opportunity to sneer at church or religion. Why, I wonder, are some people so obsessed with a religion they no longer profess to believe in?

What I find odd is the assumption of such fundamentalist non-believers that leaving religion behind is in some ways about rising to a fuller life, leaving the thickets of delusion and superstition behind for the refinements of a higher mode of living. But how can that be?

Why should it be more acceptable to believe that we are just incidental blips in the vast cosmos, living and dying without purpose or meaning, rather than that every individual human being is willed uniquely into life by God? Why should it be more acceptable that everything ends in dust rather than in a return to a fuller and more complete life with our creator and with those we love? Why should it make less sense to believe that some things are right and other things are wrong based on centuries of reflection and wisdom rather than on the morality we make up for ourselves? Why should the absence of religion be presumed to usher in a better and more refined world? Why should the existence of God be any more a delusion than the non-existence of God?

232

What the anti-religionists refuse to do is to seriously debate the contribution of religion to the individual life and to a wider society. The failures of proponents of religion are often all too clear, the achievements often hidden. Everyone knows what priests and religious did wrong; how many know or think about or even care about what they did right? Unless it's on television, someone said recently, it doesn't exist.

And what of the contribution of atheists, for example, to the good of human kind? What kind of track record do the past centuries reveal? What have non-believers done for the poor, the disadvantaged, the marginalised? What advantage can they posit for a better and braver world without the limitations of religion?

The arrogance of the anti-religionists will not allow them to accept that believers, specifically because they are believers, have made incalculable contributions to the enhancement of the lives of millions and millions of people throughout the centuries. Just one example is the thousands of Irish missionaries who in the last half century have built schools, hospitals, churches all over Africa and who did it because they felt called to do it by a God whom they believed loved and cared for them and who asked them to bring that love and care to the peoples of Africa. In Dawkins's terms, all those missionaries were deluded, but is it not the ultimate delusion to believe that getting rid of religion and its influence will usher in a better and braver world?